Eyewitness to Glory:

Discerning God's Active Presence

Moses

Eyewitness to Glory:

Discerning God's Active Presence

Moses

Mindy Ferguson

AMG PUBLISHERS

AMG Publishers | amgpublishers.com

Eyewitness Bible Studies

Eyewitness to Glory: Moses, Discerning God's Active Presence

Published by AMG Bible Studies, an imprint of AMG Publishers, Chattanooga, Tennessee (www.amgpublishers.com).

ISBN 13: 978-0-89957-910-8

First Printing—June 2014

Cover art direction by Brian Woodlief, Chattanooga, TN.

Interior design by PerfecType, Nashville, TN.

Editing and proofreading by Rick Steele

Printed in United States of America

POD

DEDICATION

This study is dedicated with love and gratitude to

the women of Fairfield Baptist Church in Cypress, Texas.

Thank you for your support, your encouragement, and your suggestions as we took this Bible study journey together.

CONTENTS

Week 4: Beyond Egypt

Week 5: Desert Rumblings

Week 6: The Tent of Meeting

Week 7: Glorious Aftereffects

Week 8: Contagious Discontent and Consequences

Week 9: Days of Wandering

Week 10: Ending Well

INTRODUCTION

Eyewitness To Glory: Discerning God's Active Presence

Moses was an eyewitness to the glory of God. Despite his sometimes crippling sense of inadequacy, he was chosen to free the Israelites from slavery in Egypt. Moses' encounters with God enabled him to overcome his insecurities and empowered him to persevere through many hardships and obstacles the people of Israel encountered along their journey. "He persevered because he saw Him who is invisible." (Hebrews 11:27)

As you see God move on behalf of His people, you will gain a greater revelation of His matchless power and holy character. The same God who was concerned about His people's suffering in Egypt and used Moses to deliver them from their oppression, is mindful of the matters that weigh heavily upon *your* heart. He is concerned about your suffering (Exodus 3:7) and in His way, and in His time, He will come to your rescue as well.

Through this study, you will watch Moses transform from a stammering, reluctant follower of God into one of the greatest leaders who ever lived. Moses' transformation was a manifestation of God's active presence. As you read Moses' legendary story, you will learn to better discern God's active presence at work in your life today. You, too, will become an eyewitness to His glory.

About This Study

The book of Exodus records the Israelites' deliverance from Egypt and their travels through the desert en route to what is known as the Promised Land. The majority of your reading will be from the book of Exodus, believed to be authored by Moses himself. The exodus story is compelling and Moses' relationship with God is inspiring. As you see God move on behalf of is people, you will gain a greater revelation of His matchless power and holy character.

Most of the lessons will take about thirty minutes to complete. Each unit is divided into five lessons designed to be done on a daily basis, five days a week. You will benefit most from doing the lessons one at a time, giving yourself time to reflect upon each lesson before moving to the next one. Be sure to begin each session with prayer, asking God to speak specifically to you through the lesson. Make notes in the margin of anything you sense God is applying directly to a situation in your life. If you are doing the study with a group, these notes will make great discussion points when you get together to discuss your homework.

All quotations are from the New International Version of the Bible, 1984 edition, unless otherwise noted. All Hebrew and Greek definitions are taken from ***Strongs Exhaustive Concordance of the Bible*** unless another source is listed.

Week 1

The Early Years

WEEK ONE DAY ONE

A Preparatory Deliverance

But God sent me ahead of you to preserve for you a remnant on earth and to save your lives by a great deliverance.

GENESIS 45:7

The book of Exodus records the Israelites' deliverance from Egypt and their travels through the desert en route to what is known as the Promised Land. Their leader was a humble man named Moses who, despite his sometimes-crippling sense of inadequacy, was chosen by God to free the Israelites from harsh conditions and oppressive slavery in Egypt.

According to Hebrews 11:27, what was the reason Moses persevered and led God's people out of Egypt?

Moses was an eyewitness to the glory of God. His encounters with our Lord enabled Him to persevere despite his personal sense of unworthiness and the many obstacles and hardships he encountered on his journey with God. Moses eventually became one of the greatest leaders who ever lived. His story will help us learn to discern God's invisible presence working around us as well.

> Moses was an eyewitness to the glory of God.

Before we begin our study of God's legendary leader, take a moment to pray. Ask God to bring His Word to life for you and to give you a greater awareness of His active presence at work in our world through Moses' story. Write a prayer on the lines below:

We will begin our study in the book of Exodus. As we open our Bibles to chapter one, the Israelites are living in Egypt, enduring mistreatment and hard labor as Pharaoh's slaves. Before we get into the heart of the Exodus story, we'll take a brief step back in time to learn a little more about the circumstances that originally brought God's people to Egypt. It all began with a young man named Joseph.

Please read Exodus 1:1–5.

The sons of Jacob (including Joseph) and their descendants eventually became known as the Israelites after Jacob's name was changed to Israel (See Genesis 32:28). The twelve sons of Israel were quite an interesting band of brothers with an intense brand of sibling rivalry. Their contention was driven by their father's obvious favoritism toward Joseph, who added fuel to his brothers' jealousy by parading around in a colorful coat given to him by their father.

Once when the brothers were grazing their father's flock a good distance from home, the resentful bunch became so fed up with Joseph's boasting, they stole his coat, threw him in a pit, and then sold him to a caravan of Ishmaelites en route to Egypt.

Disputes among siblings are common, especially when personalities differ. For instance, my husband Mark and I have two children, Brandon and Brianna. They are completely different personality types. Brandon is an introvert who likes his world orderly and calm. Brianna, on the other hand, is an adventurous extrovert who enjoys the spotlight and has an innate need to infuse every activity with an element of fun. Brianna would often parade into his room carrying whatever obnoxious toy she could find, sporting a Tupperware hat or some outrageous outfit. Brandon was rarely amused. Although they are close as adults, there were times when Brandon probably thought about shipping Brianna off (for at least a few days!) with a traveling salesman.

I suspect Joseph enjoyed irritating his brothers. Add a heaping spoonful of resentment, and this family had a recipe for disaster. Unchecked by their passive father, the Israelite boys followed through on their plot to get rid of Joseph. Once in Egypt, Joseph's troubles continued. He even spent time in an Egyptian prison for a crime he didn't commit. While there, God enabled Joseph to interpret the dreams of two of the Pharaoh's officials. Let's see what happened.

Please read Genesis 40:1–23.

After giving the interpretation to the king's cup bearer, what did Joseph ask him to do and how did he respond?

Joseph spent two years forgotten in that prison. However, the cup bearer eventually remembered Joseph, and his situation took an interesting turn.

Read Genesis 41:14–40.

How did Pharaoh describe Joseph according to verse 38?

You may be experiencing difficult circumstances in your life right now. Maybe you feel a lot like Joseph must have felt as he sat in the dingy Egyptian prison, forgotten and alone. But God had a plan for Joseph, and He has a plan for you as well. Trust Him. Regardless of how alone and forgotten you may feel, God is somehow at work in your circumstances.

But God had a plan for Joseph, and He has a plan for you as well.

Hold your place in Genesis. Then look up Ephesians 1:11. What do you learn about God's ability to bring His plans to pass?

Our God is able to orchestrate situations and bring His will to pass. He is able to empower us to perform good works on His behalf (2 Corinthians 9:8). He is able to deliver us in times of trouble (Daniel 3). But as with Joseph, sometimes His plan seems obscure and seasons of hardship can be long. In those periods, we have to trust God, even when we do not understand the purpose for our misery.

Joseph's years of suffering were finally over. He was not forgotten. By God's design, Joseph was placed into the position of prime minister of Egypt. He faithfully began filling Egypt's storehouses with life-sustaining grain until the predicted famine indeed descended upon the region. As crops dried up, people from surrounding countries journeyed to Egypt to purchase food and a familiar band of brothers was among the desperate crowd. Joseph recognized them, but they didn't recognize their brother. Joseph capitalized on the opportunity to manipulate the young men a bit, accusing them of being spies; holding one of them hostage until he had all of his brothers together at the palace. Then, overcome with emotion, Joseph revealed his true identity. Let's see how God's divine plan unfolded.

Read Genesis 45:1–11

According to verse 7, what was God's purpose for allowing Joseph to endure so many unjust and difficult circumstances?

How do you think Joseph's awareness of God's plan for deliverance impacted his feelings toward his brothers?

Now read Genesis 47:1–6. Where did the Israelites settle according to verse 6?

The Israelites settled in Goshen by the Pharaoh's invitation. Joseph could have been resentful toward his brothers. He could have sent them back to Canaan to fend for themselves. He could have moved them into the slums of Egypt. But Joseph arranged for his family to live in the best part of the land.

God is sovereign. He "works out everything in conformity with the purpose of His will" (Ephesians 1:11). James 1:2–5 tells us to "consider it pure joy" when we experience difficulties. Hardships refine us, and seasons of trial are not random. Injustices have not escaped God's almighty view. Like Joseph, that understanding causes resentment to surrender to the anticipation of a divine work of God. As Joseph calls it, "a great deliverance" (Genesis 45:7).

However, as we will discover in tomorrow's lesson, this deliverance was temporary. Joseph's descendants found themselves, once again, in need of help. The events we studied today were simply preparation for a far greater deliverance.

WEEK ONE | **DAY TWO**

Multiplying Oppression

But the more they were oppressed, the more they multiplied and spread; so the Egyptians came to dread the Israelites.

Exodus 1:12

The Israelites found refuge in Egypt. The Lord used Joseph to save his family from the severe famine and the displaced group of thankful shepherds settled in Goshen, the "best part of the land" (Genesis 47:11). God's people received favor from Egypt's king all the years Joseph was alive. However, by the time the scenes at the opening of the book of Exodus unfolded, Joseph and his brothers had died, their descendants had multiplied, and a new Pharaoh felt threatened by the growing number of Israelites living in Egyptian suburbia.

Begin today by reading Exodus 1:6–10.

What was the king's concern regarding the Israelites?

The Israelites had become so numerous Pharaoh was concerned they might join forces with an enemy and turn against him. According to the Jewish historian, Josephus, the Israelites flourished in Egypt and became wealthy "by their virtue and natural love of labor."[1] However, the new king felt threatened by this prosperous, productive group of foreigners inhabiting more and more of the "best part of the land" in Egypt.

From your experience, what usually happens when someone in a position of power feels threatened?

When my children were young, I served as treasurer on a school board. During a restructuring of the board, a new chairman took over. Many parents and staff members were resistant to his new philosophies and questioned his approach to leadership. I sat in on a staff meeting as the transition was taking place and listened in horror as the insecure chairman lashed out at the flustered staff, assaulting them with personal insults and threatening to fire anyone who complained about his new policies. Because he was insecure in his position and afraid of losing control, he became overly-controlling, issuing policies that were oppressive, and attempting to eliminate anyone who questioned him.

Egypt's king felt threatened by the Israelites, and he resolved to "deal shrewdly with them" in order to maintain control.

Read Exodus 1:11–14.

According to verse 11, what was goal of the Egyptian slave masters?

The Hebrew word translated "oppress" in this verse is ***anah*** and it carries the idea of "looking down or browbeating." According to ***Strong's Exhaustive Concordance of the Bible, anah*** means to depress, afflict, humble, and hurt. Pharaoh gave these slave masters orders to deal harshly with the Israelites and beat them down through their hard labor. Not only was the work difficult and exhausting, but God's people were mistreated as they worked.

The Hebrew word translated "oppress" in this verse is *anah* and it carries the idea of "looking down or browbeating."

As if the conditions weren't discouraging enough for the Israelites, the store cities they were forced to build honored Egyptian gods. The name Pithom meant "House of Atum," an Egyptian god known as the father of the gods. The city of Rameses was called "House of Rameses, beloved of Amon," who was another Egyptian god associated with creation power.[2]

Read Deuteronomy 4:20 below:

> ***But as for you, the Lord took you and brought you out of the iron-smelting furnace, out of Egypt, to be the people of his inheritance, as you now are.*** (NIV '84)

How were the conditions in Egypt described?

Israel had to endure the oppressive, "iron-smelting furnace" called Egypt. However, what does Exodus 1:12 tell us happened under these extreme conditions?

Most of us want to avoid discomfort, pain, or harsh treatment, but there is something extraordinary that seems to take place within us in the midst of intense circumstances. We are stretched, and we often discover inner strength we never knew existed. If you are in the middle of an intense season, remember what happened to the Israelites in Egypt and pray Exodus 1:12 over yourself. Ask God to do it again. Cry out to Him and ask Him to multiply and grow you in the midst of your "oppression." Anticipating a work of God will change your perspective and strengthen your faith.

Most of us want to avoid discomfort, pain, or harsh treatment, but there is something extraordinary that seems to take place within us in the midst of intense circumstances.

As the Israelites multiplied and grew, despite their harsh treatment, Egypt's king became more desperate to maintain control. Let's see what happened next.

Read Exodus 1:15–22.

Can you imagine the terror the Hebrew mothers must have felt as they prepared to give birth? In that culture, a woman didn't have technology to identify the gender of her baby. She went into labor wondering whether she would soon be cradling a child or carrying a coffin.

Hold your place in Exodus and read Genesis 15:13–14. What did God tell Abram hundreds of years earlier about the Israelites' years in Egypt?

____

____

God was aware of all His people were enduring in Egypt. When oppression escalated to the point where innocent babies were being murdered by a raging king, The Lord's plan to rescue His people began to unfold as an ordinary, Hebrew couple bravely sheltered their son from Pharaoh's wrath.

Read Exodus 2:1–9.

According to Exodus 6:19–20, what were the names of Moses' parents?

______________ and ______________

According to Exodus 2:2, how long did the couple hide Moses?

____

Now, can you imagine trying to hide a baby? When I brought our son home from the hospital, my colic stricken boy cried for what seemed like days straight. I remember bursting into tears one evening as Mark walked into the house from work. I had spent hours bouncing in a chair to keep Brandon from screaming.

Can you imagine trying to hide a baby?

At three months old, baby Moses' presence could no longer be kept a secret. Amram and Jochebed knew their son would soon be discovered. I imagine they spent countless, agonizing hours on their knees asking God to give them a plan, begging Him to save their boy. God faithfully answered those prayers.

According to Exodus 2:3, what did Jochebed do with baby Moses?

Perhaps the family took note of the princess's bathing schedule. Had they detected a gentle spirit in the young woman that led them to believe she would be compassionate toward their son? Was it Jochebed who thought of placing Moses in the papyrus basket? I wonder if Moses' sister, Miriam (1 Chronicles 6:3), rehearsed her line, "Shall I go and get one of the Hebrew women to nurse the baby for you?". Or, did Jochebed simply place Moses in the basket at God's direction and stand in awe as the events unfolded? There are so many questions for which we will never know the answers, but we can be certain God was working out "everything in conformity with the purpose of His will" (Ephesians 1:11) through Amram, Jochebed, and Miriam that day in Egypt.

What was the result of the family's determination to save their son?

Not only was Moses spared, he was placed back into Jochebed's arms to nurse. His courageous parents were given more than they could have hoped to receive. Moses was safe and Jochebed was paid to care for her own son. Amidst the iron-smelting furnace of Egyptian oppression, God graciously saw fit to multiply this brave family's time with their beloved Moses.

WEEK ONE **DAY THREE**

An Extraordinary Existence

Moses thought that his own people would realize that God was using him to rescue them, but they did not.

ACTS 7:25

There was something extraordinary about baby Moses. I would venture to say all mothers believe our babies are beautiful. I thought my son was the cutest baby boy ever created. But Moses' parents sensed there was something special about their baby boy.

How is Moses described in Hebrews 11:23?

Perhaps the gentle whisper of the Lord's voice (1 Kings 19:12) spoke to Amram's heart in the wee hours of the night, letting the courageous father know He had a special plan for this child. Maybe Jochebed cried out for her boy and sensed God's comforting peace like warm sunshine on a cool morning, reassuring her He had a plan.
Whatever the case, the Hebrew slaves found the gumption to defy the king's edict and God rewarded their bravery by returning Moses to Jochebed's arms. For the first time in his short life, Moses' family lived without fear of his exposure. What a glorious day that must have been at Amram's house.

Moses remained with his birth family long enough to be influenced greatly by their faith and traditions; long enough to develop a strong connection to his Hebrew heritage. "In the society of the time a baby boy was not normally weaned until the age of three, and in exceptional cases five."[3] When the time was right, Jochebed took her beloved son by his little

> Moses remained with his birth family long enough to be influenced greatly by their faith and traditions; long enough to develop a strong connection to his Hebrew heritage.

hand and walked him to the Egyptian palace to be adopted by Pharaoh's daughter. That must have been a long walk to the palace as Jochebed tried to hide her emotions from her boy while she cried out to God with each determined step. Any mother can imagine Jochebed's agony and admire her courage.

And then . . . Jochebed let him go. She released Moses from her nurturing home and placed him trustingly into the watchful care of her heavenly Father. Moses would grow up in the Egyptian palace, but I suspect Jochebed reminded her impressionable lad of the rich heritage from which he had come.

Read Acts 7:22 and note what you discover about Moses's upbringing. (You might want to hold your place in Acts, we'll read more from this passage.)

Other than this short description, Scripture is silent about the details of Moses' life in the Egyptian palace. What we do know is while Moses was living the privileged life of a royal, God's people continued to be oppressed and enslaved by the ruthless Egyptian Pharaoh Moses probably called Grandpa.

As the years passed, I wonder what thoughts Moses' family had regarding the extraordinary life of their son. Did they see him playing on the palace grounds? Did Miriam and Moses ever exchange glances? Did his sister sometimes sneak back to the bank of the Nile, hoping to catch a glimpse of Moses with his Egyptian mother? So many questions will have to remain unanswered.

Whatever his Hebrew family witnessed from outside the palace, the historian Josephus may give us some insight into what was happening within the royal Egyptian walls:

> Thermuthis ***(the Egyptian princess traditionally identified as Moses' adopted mother),*** therefore, perceiving him to be so remarkable a child, adopted him for her son, having no child of her own. And when one time she carried Moses to her father, she showed him to him, and said she thought to make him her father's successor . . . and said to him, "I have brought up a child who is of a divine form, and of a generous mind; and as I have received him from the bounty of the river, in a wonderful manner, I thought proper to adopt him for my son and the heir of thy kingdom." And when she had said this, she put

> the infant into her father's hands; so he took him, and hugged him close to his breast; and on his daughter's account, in a pleasant way, put his diadem upon his head."[4]

Keep in mind, this story is not divinely inspired Scripture, but Josephus is a well-respected historian and from reading his account, it is quite possible Moses was nurtured and educated in preparation to be successor to Pharaoh's throne. Thankfully, Moses somehow managed to keep his heart focused upon the One who is forever seated on the heavenly throne. Despite all he experienced, it also appears the mistreatment of God's people did not escape Moses' notice.

Read Exodus 2:11 – 12. How is the Hebrew described in verse 11?

Read Acts 7:23–24. How old was Moses when he killed the Egyptian?

A grown man, I imagine Moses had been watching the Egyptian slave masters mistreat his people for years. On that day, something welled up within him, and Moses could no longer stand at a distance. He could no longer remain passive.

Perhaps our resolute Egyptian prince summoned a charioteer to transport him to Pithom or Rameses. Maybe Moses saddled a horse and quietly slipped away to one of the cities. Whatever the mode of transportation, Moses arrived on the construction site that day to assess the situation. I would guess his sense of indignation grew as he thoughtfully trudged through the "iron-smelting furnace" in which his people labored.

> Moses stood and watched as an Egyptian slave driver began beating a Hebrew. And then, he lost his cool.

Moses stood and watched as an Egyptian slave driver began beating a Hebrew. And then, he lost his cool. "Glancing this way and that and seeing no one" Moses lashed out, killing the Egyptian. Recognizing his actions were wrong, Moses hid the slave driver's lifeless body in the nearest sand dune.

Moses' indignation had been warranted, but his actions had not. In a moment of anger, the hot-headed prince of Egypt had drawn a line in that sand dune. He had declared his loyalty. Moses may have been educated in all the wisdom of the Egyptians, but his heart was intricately tied to the Hebrews.

> Moses' indignation had been warranted, but his actions had not.

Read Exodus 2:13–15.

After killing the Egyptian, Moses returned to the work site the next day. This time, two Hebrews were in a scuffle and Moses' loyal heart ached as he witnessed the conflict between two of his own people. He must have wondered why the men weren't sticking together, drawing strength from one another as they endured their hardship. Yet, it's been my experience that people get grumpy when they are exhausted and overworked. Conflict was probably a common occurrence among the Hebrew slaves. Moses' privileged upbringing made the harsh plight of his fellow Hebrews a condition with which he could not relate. To complicate matters, the slaves appeared to resent his interference.

Read Acts 7: 25–29. What additional insight do you gain into Moses' thoughts as he approached the Hebrew slaves at their work site?

It appears Moses had a sense of his purpose in life. Did you notice his wording in verse 25? He "thought that his own people would realize that God was using him"? Could it be Moses had been secretly praying to God under his luxurious covers each night after the palace candles were blown out? How I wish we could learn more about the early years for our protagonist, Moses!

From his rescue by a brave Levite couple, willing to defy the King's murderous command, to the clever ruse at the bank of Nile, to his privileged education and acceptance into the royal Egyptian family, Moses certainly lived an extraordinary existence during the first forty years of his life. As we'll see in tomorrow's lesson, Moses' path took another extraordinary turn as he sat down at a well, exhausted and homeless in a sparse, desert region called Midian.

WEEK ONE **DAY FOUR**

From Prominence to Obscurity

When Pharaoh heard of this, he tried to kill Moses, but Moses fled from Pharaoh and went to live in Midian, where he sat down by a well.

EXODUS 2:15

With one rash move Moses found himself fleeing the wrath of his betrayed and powerful grandfather. God had somehow given him a glimpse of his future purpose as Israel's deliverer, and Moses got in a hurry. He assumed he was up to the task; God's gift to his fellow Hebrews. Perhaps Moses expected the weary and abused slaves to acknowledge him as their hero, to clap and cheer when he returned to the job site the next day. But just as the sight of his Egyptian garb probably incited mistrust among "his own people", the aroma of his presumptuous pride apparently conjured up some resentment.

> With one rash move Moses found himself fleeing the wrath of his betrayed and powerful grandfather.

Re-read Acts 7:25–29.

Imagine you are a Hebrew slave. You and your family have been mistreated your entire lives by the Pharaoh's slave masters. You've heard about Moses, the child who was saved from death and became a prince in the Egyptian royal family. Sadly, your own brother was murdered after taking his first breath—no miraculous salvation; only heart-rending loss. One day, the infamous Moses arrives on the scene and kills your slave-driving foreman. What thoughts or emotions might you have experienced after witnessing Moses' actions?

The Hebrew slaves not only failed to acknowledge Moses' valiant, albeit murderous, act on their behalf, they resented it. Moses had put everything on the line. He'd risked his life to reveal the secret loyalty of his heart. He'd thrown caution and wisdom to the proverbial warm, dusty wind.

What additional insight do you gain from Hebrews 11:24–25 about Moses' thoughts as he chose to betray his Egyptian adopted family?

Moses made a choice that day as he protected the Hebrew slave. He chose to give up all the treasures and pleasures the sinful, Egyptian lifestyle had to offer him and chose instead to associate himself with God's people. He had faith God would prove faithful. However, he'd forgotten one important detail. Moses forgot to inquire of the Lord and he responded from his impulsive, unrestrained human nature. As often happens when we forge ahead unchecked, attempting to do God's work in the futility of our own flesh, Moses failed. His presumptuous plans went amiss before Egyptian and Hebrew alike.

> With his true allegiance exposed, Moses was elevated to the top of Egypt's most-wanted list.

With his true allegiance exposed, Moses was elevated to the top of Egypt's most-wanted list. Prince-turned-murderer, Moses escaped with nothing but the Egyptian clothes on his back. Terrified, humiliated, and probably somewhat confused, the fugitive Moses kept running through the dry, barren desert until he ended up somewhere in the Arabian Peninsula, in a place called Midian.

Moses sat down by a well where he encountered yet another injustice. That well turned out to be God's provision for our exhausted, homeless want-to-be hero.

Read Exodus 2:15–22.

Do you feel like you just pressed the fast forward arrows on your DVD player? Remember the events described in these few verses happened over a period of years.

Peek ahead for a moment. According to Exodus 3:1, what occupation did Moses take up in Midian, and for whom did he work?

Are you wondering who this Jethro character is and what happened to Reuel? In Hebrew, the name Jethro, (or ***yithrô***) means "excellence." Reuel means "Friend of God" and seems to have been his personal name, whereas Jethro was probably his honorary title.[5] So, the man called Jethro in Exodus 3:1 is Zipporah's father, the same man referred to as Reuel in Exodus 2:18.

To gain a better understanding of the type of arrangement Moses probably made with Reuel in order to marry Zipporah, let's read about another occurrence in Scripture where a smitten traveler became the shepherd of a father's flock in order to gain the hand of his lovely daughter. Interestingly, their first encounter also occurred at a well.

Please read Genesis 29:1–20.

What arrangement did Jacob make with Laban in order to marry Rachel (v. 18)?

Moses' arrangement with Reuel was probably similar to the agreement between Jacob and Laban. Like Rachel, Zipporah was probably a young girl. "To this day girls in the region are commonly used as shepherdesses, but only to the age of puberty."[6] Perhaps Zipporah caught Moses' eye and Reuel was in need of someone to oversee his flock. Whatever conversation took place between the two men, Moses decided to stay on (as if he had a wealth of options before him), probably agreeing to shepherd Reuel's flocks in exchange for marrying his daughter Zipporah, once she reached the appropriate age for marriage.

Moses' work arrangements may have been a bit humiliating for the former prince of Egypt. According to Genesis 46:33–34, how did Egyptians feel about shepherds?

Moses topped off his dinner at the Midian priest's home that day with a large helping of humble pie as he accepted the job of a shepherd.

Moses topped off his dinner at the Midian priest's home that day with a large helping of humble pie as he accepted the job of a shepherd. We don't know much about Moses' life in Midian. We do know he'd spent forty years as prince of Egypt, enjoying all the luxuries of their culture. He had been presumptuous and tried to take his role of the Hebrews' leader too early. Could it be that some Egyptian pride had seeped into the fabric of Moses' character?

What does Matthew 23:12 tell you about the dangers of trying to exalt yourself into a leadership position?

Moses wasn't yet ready to deliver a nation. We can only assume the once prominent prince needed to be humbled before he was ready to once again be exalted to a position of significance. However, God used Moses' heroic desires to lead him to a modest place of service and preparation as a lowly shepherd of his father-in-law's flock.

A shepherd cares for the needs of his sheep (Ezekiel 34:2). He leads them to pastures to graze and to calm waters to drink (Psalm 23). A shepherd protects his flock and wards off enemies. A good shepherd will even lay down his life for his sheep, if necessary (John 10:11).

How do you think Moses' time as a shepherd in Midian might have prepared him to lead God's people later in life?

According to Acts 7:29–30, how long did Moses shepherd Reuel's flock?

Whatever the reason, after fleeing from Egypt, Moses spent the next forty years shepherding sheep in the middle of the desert. God had mighty works to perform through Moses, but first, this newly appointed shepherd appears to have needed some time in obscurity, caring for sheep in the lonely desert region of Midian.

WEEK ONE | **DAY FIVE**

Personal Application

Each week you will spend your fifth day of study reflecting upon the material you covered in the previous four lessons. I encourage you to use this format to help you review and gain additional insight that will help you apply what you are learning to your everyday life.

Application From Day 1

Despite all the injustices Joseph experienced at the hands of his brothers as well as in Egypt, he never allowed bitterness to consume him. His secret? Joseph chose to view circumstances through lenses of faith.

When our son was five years old, we discovered he was near-sighted. I will never forget the moment he tried on his first pair of glasses. His entire face lit up. He smiled, blinked several times, and then slowly looked around the optical store. As he left the building sporting his new specs, Brandon seemed amazed by the number of leaves on the trees. I was a little saddened by the realization that our boy had been unable to see the leaves on the trees prior to that day. But I was thankful our son's new glasses provided a richer, more comprehensive perspective of his world.

Joseph's perspective enabled him to maintain an unwavering trust in the sovereignty of his God. The word sovereignty conveys the supreme authority of God. Joseph believed God had a reason for allowing his hardships, knew all about the struggles he had been through, and would somehow use his experiences for a divine purpose.

Read Joseph's words in Genesis 50:19–20. How do these passages reflect Joseph's faith in God's sovereignty?

How do you usually respond when you experience hardship or endure unjust treatment? Do you tend to view your world through faith-filled lenses, believing God has a reason for allowing your suffering? Or, do you sometimes resent the trials you have suffered and wonder if God cares about your needs? Write your thoughts below:

Application from Day 2

The more the Israelite slaves were oppressed by the Egyptians, the more they multiplied and grew (Exodus 1:12). Their growth was such, Pharaoh began to see them as a possible threat to his authority; a force capable of overtaking his country. Although I never look forward to adversity, I must admit, I have often experienced substantial personal and spiritual growth during extended seasons of hardship or pain.

> Are there any circumstances in your life you are struggling to understand?

Are there any circumstances in your life you are struggling to understand? Have you ever experienced unfair treatment or felt like the innocent victim of another person's sin? If so, slip on Joseph's faith-colored glasses. How have you multiplied and grown as a result of your hardships? Have you been strengthened as a result of your pain? Have you seen evidence of God's sovereign hand, guiding you or bringing some good from your heartache or loss? Share your thoughts below:

Application From Day 3

During the first forty years of Moses' life, he lived a pampered existence as a prince in Egypt's palace, yet he seemingly grew more and more aware of the mistreatment his people were enduring as slaves. Have you ever witnessed the mistreatment of someone (or a group of people) and allowed it to continue for a time? If so, describe the situation.

Like Moses, did you eventually intervene? Assuming you did not resort to murder as Moses did, describe your choices and the outcome resulting from your actions.

Application from Day 4

Moses forgot to inquire of the Lord as he presumptuously took action and attempted to help his Hebrew people. As he fled from the wrath of Pharaoh, he found refuge in the Midian desert, raising his father-in-law's sheep. He lived in virtual obscurity as a shepherd.

According to Exodus 2:22, what name did Moses give his first born son?

The name means "expulsion" or "resident alien there"[7] and it probably conveyed Moses' keen awareness that Midian was not his home.

I feel sorry for Moses. It's been my experience, when we attempt to accomplish God's work on our time table or in our own strength, we often find ourselves in a desert; a lonely place where God's manifest presence seems absent and His divine purposes are utterly obscure.

Have you ever responded impulsively or tried to elbow your way along a desired path, only to find yourself entrenched in a lonely, humiliating desert? If so, slip back on Joseph's faith-enhancing glasses. What did you learn in your desert?

I think it is safe to assume Moses probably learned some of the same lessons during his time in Midian. It appears he acquired a pair of his own faith-colored glasses during his time as a resident alien in the desert.

Moses named his second son Eliezer, which means "God of help" (***Strong's Concordance***). According to Exodus 18:4, why did Moses choose this name?

By the birth of his second son, Moses had gained perspective. Having experienced some desert seasons a few times myself, I can attest to this: Desert stays almost always yield divine perspective.

Read Romans 8:28–29 and note what God does during desert stays:

As a way of closing this week's lessons, take a few moments to thank God for His sovereign, watchful care over your life's journey. Review your answers to the questions in today's lesson and thank Him for the good He has brought from your heartaches and troubles. Take a few moments to write a prayer of thanks, celebrating the spiritual growth and perspective you have gained along the way.

Week 2

First Encounter with God

WEEK TWO | DAY ONE

An Appointed Delay

Then the Lord said to him, "Know for certain that your descendants will be strangers in a country not their own, and they will be enslaved and mistreated four hundred years."

GENESIS 15:13

Last week we followed Moses along his rough-and-tumble journey from the spared son of Hebrew slaves, to his unlikely station as prince of Egypt; from want-to-be deliverer to Egypt's most wanted criminal; from lonely fugitive in the desert region of Midian, to resident alien, husband, father, and unassuming shepherd of his father-in-law's flock.

To refresh your memory, begin today by reading Exodus 2:11–22.

Decades passed (four to be exact) and perhaps eighty-year-old Moses wondered if his productive years were behind him. Maybe Moses and Zipporah were making plans to take over her father's business and live out the rest of their days tending sheep and enjoying grandchildren.

Meanwhile, back in Egypt, the "iron-smelting furnace" continued to grow increasingly more intense for God's people.

Please read Exodus 2:23–25.

According to verse 24, what was God mindful of as he heard the Israelites' cries and witnessed their suffering?

God promised Abraham his descendants would become a great nation and told him "all peoples on earth" would be blessed through him (Genesis 12:2–3). God also promised to give Abraham's descendants the land of Canaan, which came to be known as the Promised Land. The covenant God made with Abraham guaranteed His promise.

Please read Genesis 15:1–21. Answer the questions below about the covenant God had in mind as He heard the cries of His people in Egypt.

What promise did God make Abram (later renamed Abraham) in verses 4–5?

What promise did God make to Abram in verse 7?

After asking how he could know he would take possession of the land, what did Abram do with the animals (vv. 10–11)?

A covenant is a serious binding agreement. Typically, when a covenant like this was made, both parties would voluntarily walk between the slaughtered animals. By walking through the parts of the animal, they were symbolizing the judgment

> A covenant is a serious binding agreement.

that should befall them if they violated the agreement. They were to be cut into pieces[8] if they violated the covenant.

According to Genesis 15:17, who (or what) passed between the animal pieces?

In this case, God made a covenant with Abraham and He (represented by the smoking firepot with the blazing torch) was the only one who passed between the dead animal pieces. Isn't that amazing? Only God committed to fulfill the terms of the treaty. Only God accepted the consequences of violating the covenant. The agreement wasn't contingent upon any works of obedience on the part of Abraham. God promised the land of Canaan to Abraham's descendants, who would be as numerous as the stars in the sky.

According to Genesis 15:13–14, what did God tell Abraham (called Abram here) would happen prior to the fulfillment of the covenant?

The Israelite slaves likely felt forgotten by God.

The Israelite slaves likely felt forgotten by God. As their harsh conditions continued year after year, day after exhausting day, I imagine some of them shook their fists at God, asking the question we often ask when our foundation shakes—when a loved one is diagnosed with terminal cancer; when a child is born with Down Syndrome; when the savings account is exhausted and there are no viable employment options in sight—"Why, God? Why won't you intervene? How could you let this happen?"

Read Exodus 2:24–25 below:

> God ***heard*** their groaning and he ***remembered*** his covenant with Abraham, with Isaac and with Jacob. So God ***looked*** on the Israelites and was ***concerned*** about them (emphasis added).

God heard; He remembered; He looked, and He was concerned (vv. 24–25) about His people. Not one crack of a slave master's whip escaped the Lord's glance. Not one of the weary, discouraged slaves' tears went unnoticed. Maybe you need to know our God hears the words that have pierced your heart. He hears your cries for help. He remembers His promises. He looks upon the injustices, the tragedies, and the pain you have experienced and He sees the conditions in which you live. He is concerned about your suffering too.

> Maybe you need to know our God hears the words that have pierced your heart.

Have you ever felt overlooked by God? How are you encouraged personally by Exodus 2:24–25?

God was fully aware of His people's suffering. His inactivity did not mean He didn't care. He was concerned, and He had a plan. His chosen deliverer was being prepared for leadership in the esteemed school of the desert. God keeps His Word and His promises will never prove false. He has a time and a purpose for all things.

Read the following passages and note what you learn about God's plans:

Genesis 18:12–14:

Ecclesiastes 3:1–8:

Habakkuk 2:2–3:

If you are waiting for God to move in your circumstances, be encouraged. He truly does have a plan. Nothing is too difficult for Him, and He is concerned about the matters

> If you are waiting for God to move in your circumstances, be encouraged.

that weigh heavily upon your heart. As with the Israelites, He just might be waiting for the appointed delay to be over. Write your thoughts below.

As the sun set over both Egypt and Midian one evening, the selected time on God's divine clock arrived. Though God's deliverance had lingered, the appointed delay was over, and He was about to miraculously intervene.

You might want to pop some popcorn, grab some Twizzlers (my personal favorite) and pour a soda for Day Two's reading. God's divine plan will unfold like a captivating drama worthy of the big screen at your local theatre. The appointed delay ends, and our humble shepherd encounters unprecedented glory!

WEEK TWO DAY TWO

No Ordinary Day

So now, go. I am sending you to Pharaoh to bring my people the Israelites out of Egypt.

EXODUS 3:10

Moses had gone to sleep under the star-lit skies of Midian, just as he had each night for forty years. He probably woke up, dusted the desert grit off his well-worn sandals, and began his day as always—prodding a hungry flock of smelly sheep toward scarce patches of green underbrush. When Moses studied the rugged horizon that morning, there wasn't a hint of the miraculous. It seemed like just another ordinary, humdrum day-in-the-life of a shepherd, caring for his father-in-law's sheep.

As we begin our lesson today, please read Exodus 3:1–4.

Moses led the flock across the desert, and as he approached Mount Horeb, he saw a bush begin to burn. One would expect a dry, desert bush to be reduced to nothing but black, steaming sticks in a matter of seconds, but this bush stood strong. The mysterious flames held steady. Curious, Moses walked over to get a closer look at the "strange sight."

Moses led the flock across the desert, and as he approached Mount Horeb, he saw a bush begin to burn.

According to verse 4, when did God call to Moses from within the bush?

Moses noticed something out of the ordinary amidst the normal activity of his day, and he stopped to ponder it. He didn't just keep walking, intent on getting the sheep fed or finishing his day's work. Moses stopped. He was open to the interruption in his routine. He took the time to investigate when he noticed something extraordinary. Moses "turned aside" (KJV) and took the time to go over and see this oddity.

I can't help but wonder how I would have responded to the curious site of a blazing bush continuing to burn, unconsumed in the middle of the desert. I'd like to think I would have stopped and gone over to investigate. But based on my history, I might have continued prodding the sheep toward the far side of the mountain. I've often made the mistake of focusing too intently on my to-do list. I've missed opportunities, such as sharing a snack at the kitchen table with my daughter when she walked in the door, ready to share details from her school day. I've ducked around the corner at the grocery store in order to avoid seeing an old friend because I was concerned I might not get back to the house early enough to get the last load of laundry folded before heading to my son's basketball game. Sadly, if I were Moses it might have taken more than a single burning bush to get my attention.

I can't help but wonder how I would have responded to the curious site of a blazing bush continuing to burn, unconsumed in the middle of the desert.

How do you respond when something out of the ordinary interrupts your routine? If you were Moses, would you have immediately gone over to take a closer look or, based on past experience, do you think you might have continued right on walking busily to the nearest patch of green brush so you could mark ***feed the sheep*** off your to-do list?

On my journey with God, I've discovered that when the source of an interruption is the Creator Himself, the purpose usually involves a needed correction or some sort of change in direction. I have come to realize I need to be listening and watching for God's activity around me. I want to be more open to interruptions. I need to remember that disruptions to my schedule are sometimes divine appointments.

I have come to realize I need to be listening and watching for God's activity around me.

Let's see what God had to say to Moses during this unexpected divine appointment in the middle of the Midian desert.

Please read Exodus 3:5–8.

According to verse 5, why did God tell Moses to remove his sandals?

The blazing bush was probably just a thorny, pale desert shrub. I imagine the sheep had trampled the ground around it and nibbled on its buds as they passed just moments earlier. But as the flames of glory ignited within its bristly branches, the shrub and the ground on which it stood became distinctive, set apart—holy. The transforming presence of the one and only holy, omnipotent, God is what made this bush and this ground extraordinary.

It isn't clear exactly why God told Moses to remove his sandals. But in the culture and time, the removal of one's sandals was regarded as a mark of respect.[9] (Even today, Muslims remove shoes before entering mosques.) One thing is clear: the Lord pierced through the monotony of the desert and called Moses by name. He had a heavenly message, and as Moses "turned aside," God made sure He had Moses' full attention.

When the soles of the terrified shepherd's calloused feet sank into the hot desert sand, Moses probably had a sense life as he knew it was about to change. I imagine his heart beating quickly as he waited to see what God would do next.

According to verse 6, what was the first thing God wanted Moses to know?

To reinforce the reason God may have chosen to identify Himself in this particular manner, please read God's message to Moses' ancestor, Jacob, in Genesis 35:11 – 13. What promise did God make Jacob in verse 12?

Now Read Genesis 50:24. What did Joseph remind his brothers (the Israelites) just before he died?

God identified himself to Moses as the same God who made a covenant with Abraham; the same God who promised Abraham, Isaac, and Jacob He would one day bring their descendants into the promised land of Canaan; the same God who told Abraham his people would be enslaved and mistreated for four hundred years.

Look back at Genesis 15:14. What did God promise to do after his people's time of enslavement was over?

Now that you have the same context Moses had as he stood covering his face before the fiery bush, read Exodus 3:9– 11.

When God told Moses He had "come down" to rescue His people, I imagine the former prince was elated. God said it was finally time for His people to make their way to the "good and spacious" Promised Land. Our former deliverer-want-to-be probably whispered an "hallelujah" under His breath. God was breaking the silence, righting the wrongs, and making good on His promise.

But according to verse 10, how did God plan to implement His divine rescue mission?

Moses was shaken out of his awestruck silence. Thoughts probably raced in his head, ***What? Me? You want who? Go back?*** Moses managed to gather himself enough to simply say, "Who am I?" (vs.11).

God had a plan. A divine interruption was necessary. With the igniting of a common desert bush, the desire God placed upon Moses' heart so many years earlier was about to come to pass. Moses' time in the desert had prepared him and Jethro would have to find another shepherd. The Lord would use Moses to rescue the Hebrew slaves in Egypt (Acts 7:25). This time God had commissioned Moses, and the weary Israelites would recognize him as their divinely-appointed deliverer.

> God had a plan. A divine interruption was necessary.

The delay was over. The Israelites would soon be free. The sun may have risen in Midian just like any other morning, but this was certainly no ordinary day in the life of this humble shepherd.

WEEK TWO DAY THREE

Wavering Faith

But Moses said to God, "Who am I, that I should go to Pharaoh and bring the Israelites out of Egypt?"

Exodus 3:11

We last saw Moses standing barefoot in the desert sand, covering his face as the Lord said, "So now, go. I am sending you to Pharaoh to bring my people the Israelites out of Egypt" (Exodus 3:10).

According to Exodus 3:11, how did Moses respond?

Read Exodus 3:12. What did God say would be a sign to Moses that indeed God is the one who sent him to Egypt?

God told Moses to go. Only after his rescue mission would the reluctant leader-to-be know God had been the One to send him. His confirmation would come as he and the Israelites gathered there at Mount Horeb to worship. That's not exactly the answer Moses was hoping for. Surely God could give him a sign ***before*** he returned to Egypt—before he risked his life confronting Pharaoh; before he made a fool out of himself attempting to set the Israelites free. But God wanted Moses to exercise faith.

> God told Moses to go.

How does Hebrews 11:1 define faith?

Faith requires action. Our confirmation of God's presence and empowerment usually comes only after we have obediently followed His instructions.

> Faith requires action.

I experienced this first hand when I, as a fairly new member of my home church, was approached about serving as the Women's Ministry Director. I had been involved in women's ministry elsewhere for years and loved working with women (still do!). But, between my responsibilities at the ministry and our family business, my proverbial plate was quite full. After praying about the possibility of accepting the responsibility for about a week, I declined. However, the same night I turned down the position, I had a restlessness deep in my spirit that I couldn't shake. I told my husband I didn't feel completely at peace with my decision and didn't know what I should do. He looked me straight in the eyes and asked if I wanted to hear his opinion. It was the first time I realized I hadn't asked.

"Of course I do," I replied. "I'm sorry I didn't ask."

Mark then matter-of-factly stated, "I think you are the right person and I think you need to talk to the pastors about your concerns."

I immediately emailed the executive pastor, apologized for being wishy-washy, and asked to meet with him and the senior pastor about the position. We met, and the two of them had an answer for each of my objections. I wasn't completely sure I was making the right decision, but I agreed to take on the responsibility for one year and see how it went. It wasn't until the new women's ministry team was gathered at our first leadership retreat (about eleven months later), worshiping and praising God in a small beach house we had rented for the weekend that I recognized I had indeed made the right decision. God had created an amazing team of unified, servant leaders who were committed to glorifying Him and working together as a team to meet the needs of the women at our church. It was an overwhelming moment I will never forget. I served as their Women's Ministry Director for three years and saw God accomplish far more than I could ever have accomplished on my own. The proof of His empowerment was evident in the results.

God often necessitates action before He confirms we've heard him correctly. He requires His people to respond with faith—". . .being sure of what we hope for [His presence and empowerment] and certain of what we do not [yet!] see [an outcome that glorifies Him]." However, our human natures long to know detailed steps before we embark on a task.

God often necessitates action before He confirms we've heard him correctly.

Moses wanted to know the details too. As a matter of fact, he had quite a few questions swirling around in his mind as he began to absorb the enormity of the task for which he was being commissioned. With the unfiltered candor of someone thinking out loud, Moses boldly shared his concerns with His Lord. Let's continue eavesdropping on their conversation.

Please read Exodus 3:13–15.

Moses was afraid that his fellow Israelites might not believe him. After all, they had questioned his motives the last time he reached out to help. So Moses essentially asked God the first question he thought might come up, "What if they ask your name, Lord? Then what do I tell them"?

According to verse 14, how did God identify Himself?

The name "I AM" in Hebrew means God is and will be present in your situation. Isn't that an amazing response? In other words, God said to Moses, "I—the covenant God of Abraham, Isaac, and Jacob—AM 'truly he who exists and who will be dynamically present then and there in the situation to which I am sending you.' "[10] Isn't that what we want to know as we embark on frightening, unchartered territory? Details may be allusive, but we can rest assured the "I AM" is there. He exists and when we obey Him, He will be dynamically present in the situation with us. That's what Moses experienced as he laid his fears and objections before the Lord. He received a personal promise of God's presence and power.

Details may be allusive, but we can rest assured the "I AM" is there.

Let's see what God tells Moses next. Please read Exodus 3:16–22.

Moses was given step-by-step instructions and told the initial response he could expect from Pharaoh. What did God say would eventually compel Pharaoh to let the Israelites go (vs. 19–20)?

God would be dynamically present. Moses would have some ups and downs, but the Lord's mighty hand would eventually compel Pharaoh to let his people go. For what more could Moses have asked? But God wasn't finished. Read Exodus 4:1–9.

I'm so encouraged by the Lord's patience with Moses. He offered not one, not two, but three miraculous signs to validate Moses' story. God was gracious and compassionate toward His reluctant, up-and-coming leader.

How does Joel 2:13 describe our Lord?

The exchange between the Lord and Moses certainly confirms the prophet's description. God was amazingly gracious, slow to anger, and abounding in unconditional love for Moses. He is patient with us too. But just as often happens to us, Moses was overwhelmed by his fear and doubt; worked up by the demands of his divine assignment. So much so, I think he forgot with whom he was speaking.

Read Exodus 4:10–17.

How did Moses' objections impact the Lord (v. 14)?

God's patience does not signify indifference.

God's patience does not signify indifference. "Without faith it is impossible to please Him" (Hebrews 11:6). The Lord's anger "burned against Moses" for his lack of trust. However, He graciously allowed Moses to choose a less-than-His-best plan—a compromise (that we will see brings consequences later). Aaron would be Moses' spokesman. Moses would tell Aaron what to say and Aaron would relay it to the people and to Pharaoh. It was not God's best, but God's purposes would still prevail. And before Moses rushed off to tell his father-in-law he needed a leave of absence, God told Moses to take the staff in ***his*** hands. He might not have to speak, but he ***would*** have to perform the miraculous signs. It was a compromised mission strategy for a frightened man of wavering faith.

WEEK TWO | DAY FOUR

Tales of Two Sons

And I told you, "Let my son go, so he may worship me." But you refused to let him go; so I will kill your firstborn son."

Exodus 4:23

I relate to Moses as he voiced his fearful objections to the Lord's call. I've acted like he did more than once in my journey with God. I, too, have never been eloquent and can be slow of speech and tongue. Like the introverted Moses, I struggle to speak well when I'm caught off guard or asked a question for which I was unprepared. Moses asked God just about every question he could imagine would come up during his talk with the elders of Israel. He felt inadequate and was concerned they wouldn't believe God had truly appeared to him. I understand Moses' need to talk through all of those questions so he could prepare his answers.

Like the introverted Moses, I struggle to speak well when I'm caught off guard or asked a question for which I was unprepared.

Begin today by re-reading Exodus 4:10–17.

What was the Lord's response to Moses' concerns according to Exodus 4:11–12?

God knew exactly how Moses would deliver His message and as the Creator of all things, He was certainly capable of choosing a leader. The fearful deliverer-to-be was inadvertently questioning God's judgment. We all have weaknesses of some sort, but when our Creator assigns us to a task, we can rest assured He will empower us to accomplish the work.

What weaknesses do you possess that cause you to feel inadequate or unqualified for a divine assignment?

What does 2 Corinthians 12:9 tell us about God's power in times of weakness?

After their lengthy dialogue, the Lord sent Moses off with specific instructions. Aaron would be Moses' mouthpiece before the elders of Israel and before Pharaoh. The two brothers would be a team. The plan was a compromise that would eventually bring consequences for both Moses and the Israelites. However, despite all the humble shepherd's doubts and insecurities, God still chose him to lead the Hebrew slaves out of Egypt.

Before starting his mission, Moses needed to relay the unexpected news to his family. Please read Exodus 4:18–23.

Look back at Exodus 3:19–20. What did the Lord say about Pharaoh?

According to Exodus 4:21, what did God say he would do to Pharaoh's heart?

God told Moses in advance that he would be endowed with the ability to release plague after plague upon the Egyptians. However, the obstinate Pharaoh would refuse to cooperate and ultimately, God would let the evil king endure the consequences. He would let Pharaoh have his way. The Lord would eventually withhold mercy and "harden" the evil king's heart. After nine lesser plagues, God would punish Pharaoh by bringing a final pestilence on the king and his people known as the Plague of the Firstborn.

After nine lesser plagues, God would punish Pharaoh by bringing a final pestilence on the king and his people known as the Plague of the Firstborn.

According Exodus 4:22–23, what was the reason God would choose this particular course of action?

(Hold your place in Exodus) Now Read Genesis 49:3 and Deuteronomy 21:15–17 and note what you learn about the significance of a firstborn son:

A firstborn son had special honor in a family. He received a double portion of the father's wealth, received special privileges, and was considered a sign of the father's strength. The Lord called the nation of Israel His firstborn son. In other words, the people of Israel were "first in rank . . . with all the rights, privileges, and responsibilities of a firstborn."[11] Pharaoh refused to let God's firstborn go and worship Him. Therefore, Pharaoh (and ultimately all the Egyptians) would lose his firstborn.

A firstborn son had special honor in a family.

Read Exodus 4:24–26.

This is a very strange story, isn't it? God sends Moses on this paramount mission, promises to equip and empower him, then suddenly we read the Lord was about to kill him. But it appears Moses had failed to circumcise his son (probably referring to his firstborn).

God instituted circumcision after making his covenant with Abraham. Read Genesis 17:11–14, and note why Moses' failure to circumcise his son would be significant:

Moses had failed to obey God's command. His son didn't bear the sign of the covenant. Let's use our imaginations for a moment and pretend we are peering through the window of Moses' lodging place. Moses is in bed, gravely ill. The Lord tells Moses his illness (and impending death) are due to his failure to circumcise his son. Based upon Moses' previous conversations with God, I'm guessing he, perhaps, made excuses. Maybe his wife Zipporah, of a different culture, thought the act was barbaric and cruel. Maybe a less-than-courageous Moses had let his wife's protests stop him from carrying out the sacred act.

Moses had failed to obey God's command. His son didn't bear the sign of the covenant.

As we watch through the window, Moses is arguing with the Lord and, as before, God's anger burns against him. God reminds Moses that his uncircumcised son must be "cut off from his people" (Genesis 17:14) and because of the former shepherd's willful disobedience, Moses will die if he doesn't rectify the situation. Moses may be passive, but Zipporah springs into action. Her family is in trouble. She runs across the room to get the flint knife out of their sheepskin knapsack. Despite her boy's screams, she completes the gory act. Nothing feels sacred about this bloody, brutal ritual. She sees Moses' feet sticking out of the covers and remembers the story of removing his sandals to stand barefoot on holy ground. Desperate for the Lord to mercifully honor her attempt to defuse His wrath, Zipporah touches her firstborn's bloody foreskin to Moses' calloused feet. Venting her anger and disgust at what she considers a detestable act, Zipporah says with teeth clenched, "Surely you are a bridegroom of blood to me." The room, a flurry of bloody activity just moments earlier, falls silent.

I imagine it happened something like that, anyway. According to Exodus 4:26, how did the Lord respond?

The Lord relented. He honored Zipporah's desperate act to save her family. The crisis was averted and the mission could move forward. Let's return to our story and see what happened as Moses began his trip back to his old stomping grounds in Egypt.

Read Exodus 4:27–28.

Moses filled Aaron in on the events of the previous days; the blazing bush, the Lord's voice, the holy ground, and the unlikely mission. He relayed his doubts and told Aaron about the miraculous signs. Moses shared God's plan to free the Israelites.

> The Lord relented. He honored Zipporah's desperate act to save her family. The crisis was averted and the mission could move forward.

Moses and Aaron made plans to gather the elders. Aaron would speak, and Moses would tell him what to say. They would be a dynamic team. They had God's assurance that "the elders of Israel would listen" (Exodus 3:18) and Pharaoh would not. In the end, Pharaoh's firstborn son would die to free God's firstborn. The king would finally relent and let Israel go (Exodus 3:20). With their orders clear, our lesson ends today as the two commissioned sons of Amram, accompanied by Moses' family, load up their camels and head determinedly into the dusty, desert horizon toward Egypt.

WEEK TWO | DAY FIVE

Personal Application

Application for Day One:

During the Israelites four hundred-year-stay in the "iron-smelting furnace" of Egypt, God's people cried out to him for deliverance. Throughout those long years, God was aware of their suffering. Look again at Exodus 2:24–25 below:

> God ***heard*** their groaning and he ***remembered*** his covenant with Abraham, with Isaac and with Jacob. So God ***looked*** on the Israelites and was ***concerned*** about them (emphasis added).

Reflect for a moment on a time when you endured a long season of suffering. Describe the circumstances below in five words or less:

During that period, what is it that you most want to know God heard?

What is one thing you want to know He saw?

How do Psalm 33:13–14 and Malachi 3:16 encourage you?

> God is everywhere. He listens to your conversations and remembers how you've honored His name.

God is everywhere. He is aware of everything that takes place on earth. He sees all and knows all. He listens to your conversations and remembers how you've honored His name. He is aware of everything you have been through, and He always keeps His Word. You can rest assured; He is concerned about your suffering.

Write a prayer on the lines below. Tell your God how you felt during the scenario listed above. Praise Him for His omnipresence (presence everywhere at all times). Thank Him for His concern. Pour out your heart before Him. Your God is looking down at you right now and, as a woman who fears Him, He will listen to your prayer.

Application for Day Two:

Although God is present everywhere all the time, He sometimes chooses to make His presence known. This is what is called a manifestation of God's presence. To manifest means "to make visible, clear, manifest, known."[12] When God chooses to make His presence or activity clear to us, we experience the glory of God.

The bush that burned in the desert of Midian wasn't significant. Moses had probably passed by that ordinary shrub many times. The sheep may have nibbled at its buds. Lizards may have perched on its branches. It was probably just a thorny, pale desert bush. But when God chose to make Himself visible through the fire, it was the manifestation of His presence that made the bush (and the ground around it) holy, set apart, and special.

Perhaps as you read this you feel a lot like a dehydrated, pale desert bush. Nothing special. You are just an ordinary woman serving your family in an average home. You do your everyday work, unappreciated and unnoticed by a world enamored with celebrities, wealth, and crass thrill seekers. But, if you are a believer in Jesus Christ, you are not ordinary at all. Like the average bush ablaze with a mysterious, transforming fire, you have the Spirit of our Lord burning within you and His presence makes you holy, set apart, and extraordinary.

Although God is present everywhere all the time, He sometimes chooses to make His presence known. This is what is called a manifestation of God's presence.

What does 1 Corinthians 3:16 tell you about the Holy Spirit?

Read Colossians 1:27 below and underline what we're told is a mystery to us:

To them God has chosen to make known among the Gentiles the glorious riches of this mystery, which is Christ in you, the hope of glory. (NIV 84)

God is present with us, mysteriously living within each of us as a believer in Jesus Christ. He enables us to experience His power through His Spirit (Acts 1:8); He makes Himself visible as He works in our world through His Spirit (1 Corinthians 12:7–11). He makes His will known as He convicts us of sin (John 16:8) and speaks to us by His Holy Spirit (John 10:4, 16:13). We experience the glory of God whenever He makes Himself known to us through the activity of His Holy Spirit.

Application for Day Three:

When God told Moses He was sending him to Egypt, Moses panicked. The frightened shepherd stammered, stated his objections, shared his insecurities, and even bluntly asked God to send someone else to do it (Exodus 4:13). But despite all of his objections, Moses was God's choice to lead His people out of Egypt.

God is present with us, mysteriously living within each of us as a believer in Jesus Christ.

What current circumstances are causing you to feel frightened, alone, or insecure?

Place your feet in Moses' sandy footprints for a moment. What objections would you raise as God tells you to move forward?

What current circumstances are causing you to feel frightened, alone, or insecure?

As Moses wrestled with fear, God identified Himself by the name, I AM. When we choose to obey our Lord, He, as the "I AM," will be dynamically present in our circumstances. That's what Moses discovered as he placed his fears and objections before the Lord. He received a personal promise of God's presence and power.

Look back at your objections listed above. Fill in the blanks below and then read it out loud:

God says, "I—the covenant God of Abraham, Isaac, and Jacob—AM truly He who exists and who will be dynamically present then and there ______________________ (state your circumstances), ______________________(your name)."

Do you believe it? Like Moses, you may still experience some fear, but you can rest in the knowledge that the "I AM" will go before you, be with you, and infuse His power into your circumstances.

Application for Day Four:

Moses encountered God's manifest presence in the burning bush and was commissioned to lead the Israelites out of Egypt. Despite his perceived lack of qualifications, God was unwilling to "send someone else" to lead His people. Moses, accompanied by his family and his brother Aaron, embarked on a great adventure as God's chosen messenger and ultimate leader.

As we close the week, I'd like to share some wording that caught my attention from the passages we read this week.

Re-read Exodus 4:18–20.

How is the staff Moses took along on the journey to Egypt described (v. 20)?

____

Now look at Exodus 4:27. How is the mountain described?

____

Moses had probably carried that staff for years, using it to prod sheep, kill desert creatures, and support his weary legs at the end of a long day. But as God revealed His power through that staff, "the ordinary became extraordinary by virtue of its use in the service of God"[13]. Mount Horeb, once just an ordinary mountain somewhere in the Arabian Peninsula, was now called the "mountain of God" because the Lord had chosen to reveal His manifest presence there in the burning bush.

Look at Deuteronomy 33:1. How is Moses described at the end of his life?

____

Moses was slow of speech and tongue (Exodus 4:10). He murdered a man at the age of forty (Exodus 2:12). He'd spent forty years as a fugitive, shepherding his father-in-law's sheep. However, by virtue of his service to God, Moses was known at his death as "Moses, the man of God."

Regardless what you've done in your past, you also have a new identity as a servant of Christ.

Write 2 Corinthians 5:17 on the lines below:

> Regardless what you've done in your past, you also have a new identity as a servant of Christ.

____

____

Like Moses, you might have lived many years feeling ordinary or unimportant. Your life might be filled with regrets and mistakes. Your occupation may not seem significant to the world. But when you become a believer in Jesus and the Holy Spirit takes up residency with you; when you dedicate your life to serving our Lord, you—just an ordinary woman—can be remembered as a woman of God.

As a way of closing, fill in your name below. By virtue of your use in the service of your Lord, you are now:

______________________________ (Your Name), the woman of God.

Week 3

Petitions and Plagues

WEEK THREE DAY ONE

Futile Petitions and Misplaced Blame

And they said, "May the LORD look upon you and judge you! You have made us a stench to Pharaoh and his officials and have put a sword in their hand to kill us."

EXODUS 5:21

Moses and his family arrived in Egypt. The former-prince had been gone for forty years. We aren't told if Amram and Jochebed were still alive (Exodus 4:18). If so, I wonder what that reunion might have been like. Did the elderly couple cry as they embraced their grandsons for the first time? Did Jochebed and Zipporah spend the afternoon in the kitchen preparing a special celebration meal? Did Moses immediately share the details of his encounter at the burning bush with his father or did he ease into the topic after an hour of small talk? Scripture is silent about the details of any reunion, but the family certainly had a lot to talk about.

As our reading begins today, Moses and Aaron are getting right down to business, gathering the elders of Israel together, just as they were instructed to do.

Please read Exodus 4:29–31.

Things were going along according to plan. The Israelites believed Moses, just as the Lord said they would. The people were encouraged by God's concern and the entire group bowed before Him as they ended their meeting with an intense time of reverent worship. Unfortunately, however, Mission Deliverance would soon encounter some predicted complications.

Things were going along according to plan. The Israelites believed Moses, just as the Lord said they would. Unfortunately, however, Mission Deliverance would soon encounter some predicted complications.

Read Exodus 5:1–5.

According to verse 2, how did Pharaoh respond to the brothers' request?

Aaron relayed God's message saying, "the God of Israel says: 'Let my people go.' " Egyptians believed in numerous gods and goddesses. There was one for almost every situation or place.[14] In fact, Pharaoh himself was considered a god. There were probably numerous statues of the king gracing the Egyptian skyline. He was the big chief. The head honcho. What he said was law. He was accustomed to people doing whatever **he** told them to do. Pharaoh scoffed, "Who is this LORD? I've never heard of him so why should I obey him?" The arrogant king was unimpressed and unaffected.

As Moses and Aaron protested, Pharaoh abruptly brushed off their concerns. Irritated, the ruler brought up the only scenario that concerned him—the work his slaves would miss if he granted Moses' request. Pharaoh dismissed the pair, but it appears he continued to stew over their request long after the brothers left. Enraged by the Hebrews' audacity to request time off, the fuming Pharaoh sent a message to the slave drivers and Hebrew foremen.

Let's see what happened next. Please read Exodus 5:6–9.

What did Pharaoh order the slave drivers and foremen to do?

Make the labor harder? They already felt like they were working in an "iron-smelting furnace." The Israelites had listened and believed Moses and Aaron. They had witnessed the staff turn into a snake. The weary slaves had been told the Lord was concerned about their suffering. They had just worshipped together and praised God for sending Moses to deliver them. The slaves were expecting freedom. The foremen, Hebrews themselves, had to deliver the distressing news.

Read Exodus 5:10–16.

The Hebrews went from the furnace to the fire. Conditions weren't just worse, they were impossible. Frenzied, they scattered all over Egypt, gathering whatever "stubble" they could find in an attempt to make the proper number of bricks. But regardless how hard they worked, the men weren't able to meet their quota. The Hebrew foremen were beaten and interrogated. Bewildered by the changes, the overwhelmed and confused crew tried to reason with Pharaoh.

The Hebrews went from the furnace to the fire. Conditions weren't just worse, they were impossible.

Read Exodus 5:17–21.

With curled lips and eyes ablaze, the angry Pharaoh snarled out accusations against the Hebrew people. Suddenly, the confused Israelite foremen gained clarity . . . ***It was Moses!*** His meeting with the Egyptian king hadn't brought freedom, it brought greater oppression.

According to verse 21, how did the foremen respond to Moses and Aaron?

Moses had been on an emotional mountaintop after his meeting with the elders. They'd all worshiped together and thought they would be heading out of Egypt by sunset. Now Moses was quickly descending that mountaintop. He had done everything God commanded him to do, but the situation was getting worse, not better.

Have you ever been in a situation where you did your best to obey God's commands and honor Him with your choices, yet circumstances seemed to get progressively worse, not better? If so, give a brief description of the event:

What did you learn from that experience?

I imagine Moses probably felt a lot like you did as circumstances in Egypt went from bad to worse. So what did Moses do? He went back to the One who put him in this position in the first place.

Please read Exodus 5:22–23 and summarize Moses' protests in your own words?

Pharaoh blamed the "lazy" workers; the foremen blamed Moses, and now Moses blamed God. In essence, Moses said, "See God. I told you I wasn't the right person. You are the one who insisted I do this. Is this why you sent me, to fall on my face in front of everyone? I told you I cannot do this! And ***you*** have not rescued your people at all."

Isn't that how we often react when we encounter perceived failure? We look for someone to blame and sometimes, we even blame God, assuming He has let us down.

Has there ever been a time when you felt like God let you down? If so, how can you relate to Moses' questions in verses 22–23?

Look again at God's words to Moses back at the burning bush (Exodus 3:18–20). What did God tell Moses would happen?

God was clear. Pharaoh wouldn't budge until the Lord struck the Egyptians with "all the wonders" He planned to perform among them.

God was clear. Pharaoh wouldn't budge until the Lord struck the Egyptians with "all the wonders" He planned to perform among them. Moses' petitions before Pharaoh were predicted to fail. God knew the Israelites would blame Moses, and He was working out everything in conformity with the purpose of His will (Ephesians 1:11). He had a plan. However, like us, Moses wanted instant results. He'd forgotten the plan, and he wanted someone to blame. However, Moses would soon discover that the Lord can handle our misplaced blame. Thankfully, he would also learn that when our heartfelt petitions are presented to God, we can rest assured they are never futile.

WEEK THREE DAY TWO

Covenant Keeper

I appeared to Abraham, to Isaac and to Jacob as God Almighty,
but by my name the LORD I did not make myself known to them.

EXODUS 6:3

We last saw Moses before the Lord, exasperated over his mission's lack of results. Pharaoh was furious at the Hebrew people who were, in turn, angry at Moses. From Moses' perspective, the situation was dismal at best. He'd done everything the Lord told him to do, and circumstances were worse than when he arrived.

We last saw Moses before the Lord, exasperated over his mission's lack of results.

Begin today by reading Exodus 5:22—6:1. How did the Lord respond to Moses' frustration?

God could handle Moses' discouragement. He didn't discipline Moses for his misplaced blame and obvious frustration. God was compassionate and allowed Moses to share his raw emotions, responding with words of encouragement rather than condemnation. In essence, God said, "Don't you worry Moses, the great I AM is about to show you how He is dynamically present in your circumstances. Watch what I am about to do to Pharaoh."

Let's see what God said next. Please read Exodus 6:2–5 and then look carefully at the verses below:

> God also said to Moses, "I am ***the LORD***. I appeared to Abraham, to Isaac and to Jacob as ***God Almighty***, but by my name ***the LORD*** I did not make myself known to them (emphasis added). (Exodus 6:2–3)

The name for God translated here as "God Almighty" is ***El-Shaddai***. It relates to an all-sufficient, all-powerful God who is able to provide everything we need. The Israelites' forefathers had experienced God's provision and His power countless times. They not only knew His name, El-Shaddai, they had come to know Him as their all sufficient God.

Think back over the past year. In what ways have you personally experienced (come to know) God as El-Shaddai?

Moses and the Hebrew people knew the Lord as God Almighty! God had provided courageous parents for Moses, a privileged upbringing, and a place of refuge when he fled Egypt. Moses also knew God had positioned Joseph as prime minister in Egypt hundreds of years earlier to provide for His people during the seven-year famine. Moses had heard about how God provided a child for the elderly Abraham and his formerly barren wife, Sarah. He also knew about the covenant God made with Abraham; a covenant passed along to Abraham's descendants. The promise had been given, but not yet fulfilled. The great I AM was about to fulfill that promise.

The situation in Egypt had reached its bleakest point. The oppression of God's people had escalated to unbearable proportions. Amidst these seemingly impossible circumstances, God told Moses His people would not only come to know Him as El Shaddai (their provider), but they would come to know Him as The LORD.

Look back at Exodus 3:15. By what name did God say He wanted to be remembered from generation to generation?

Let's explore the meaning of this name. The LORD in Hebrew, listed in all caps in our Bibles, is Yahweh. It is the proper name for God and is associated with the fulfillment of His covenant. God made a covenant with Abraham. He told Abraham his descendants would be enslaved and mistreated for four hundred years, but God promised to then rescue them and punish the nation they served as slaves. Then one day they would return to Canaan and He would give them that land as their own country.

The LORD in Hebrew, listed in all caps in our Bibles, is Yahweh. It is the proper name for God and is associated with the fulfillment of His covenant.

God was about to make good on His promise, and in the process, His people would discover Yahweh isn't just a God of history; He isn't just a promise giver; Yahweh—the great I AM—is an active, dynamically present covenant keeper.

God was about to make good on His promise.

The Lord went on to explain the actions He would take to reveal Himself as that active and present covenant keeper. On the lines below, fill in the blanks from Exodus 6:6–8 to identify the seven actions God had planned:

I will ________________ you out from under the yoke of the Egyptians (v. 6).

I will ________________ you from being slaves to them (v. 6)

I will ________________ you with an outstretched arm and with mighty acts of judgment. (v. 6)

I will ________________ you as my own people, and (v. 7)

I will ________________ your God (v. 7).

I will ________________ you to the land I swore with uplifted hand to give to Abraham, to Isaac and to Jacob (v. 8).

I will ________________ it to you as a possession (v. 8). I am THE LORD.

In the course of this study, we will watch God fulfill many of those promises to His people. God not only intended to free His people from bondage in Egypt, He planned to lovingly identify them as His people and bring the nation into intimate fellowship with Him as their God. He then intended to fulfill his covenant promise to Abraham by bringing the Israelites to Canaan and giving the land to them, just as He said He would do.

According to Exodus 6:9, how did the Israelites respond to God's divine plan to reveal Himself as their dynamically present covenant keeper and what was the reason for their response?

Maybe you feel a little like the Israelites as you read this lesson. Your life has been difficult for a long time and you feel like God hasn't noticed.

Don't we have the most difficulty believing our God is Yahweh (a dynamically present promise keeper) when we are most discouraged? Maybe you feel a little like the Israelites as you read this lesson. You know the stories in Scripture and are absolutely convinced those accounts are true. You know God is powerful and able to meet your needs. But your life has been difficult for a long time and you feel like God hasn't noticed. The Lord you've heard about all your life seems like a distant, abstruse deity who works in other people's lives, but just doesn't seem active or present in your circumstances.

Read Psalm 139:1–16 and note the assurances you have that God is present in your current circumstances:

You may feel forgotten, but Yahweh knows you intimately. You have been uniquely created. The Lord watches over you and He will keep His Word. I'm praying right now that through the course of this study, you will come to know God more fully as Yahweh—***your*** dynamically-present promise keeper.

> You may feel forgotten, but Yahweh knows you intimately.

Moses stood before the Lord that day discouraged and confused, but God encouraged him by basically saying, "I am about to show you and my people that I indeed care. I AM a dynamically present God who is worthy of your trust. I AM Yahweh, and you are about to experience me as your covenant-keeping God."

In Day Three we will read through the plagues that Yahweh brought upon the Egyptians as He began the process of fulfilling His promise. Allow a little extra time. It will be time well-spent as you witness those miraculous manifestations of God's awe inspiring glory.

WEEK THREE DAY THREE

Enlightening Glory

"Tomorrow," Pharaoh said. Moses replied, "It will be as you say, so that you may know there is no one like the Lord *our God."*

Exodus 8:10

Yesterday as we observed Moses sharing his discouragement and confusion, we also saw God encourage him. The lover of Moses' soul told his chosen deliverer exactly what He intended to do on behalf of His people, and He assured Moses the Israelites would come to know Him as Yahweh—the dynamically present promise keeper. Interestingly, through the passages we'll study together today in Day Three, we'll observe the Egyptians also recognized Yahweh as a dynamically present God.

Begin today by reading Exodus 6:28—7:7.

Moses just couldn't let the faltering lips objection go, could he? Thankfully, God did. He simply restated His intentions (once again) and commanded the reluctant leader and his designated speaker to move forward with the divine plan.

Let's see what happened as the obedient pair performed the first miracle before Egypt's hostile king. Please read Exodus 7:8–13.

The Egyptian magicians may have been able to conjure up similar results with their fancy allusions, but the real-deal-miracle proved its superiority by swallowing up those inferior reptiles. However, as the Lord said, the cynical Pharaoh was unimpressed and refused to listen.

Look back at Exodus 4:21. To whom did God give the power to perform wonders in Egypt?

Moses was so focused on his weaknesses that despite God's repeated assurances of His power and reminders of Pharaoh's response, Moses struggled to believe God could work through a man who is slow of speech and speaks with faltering lips. Interestingly, God graciously came up with a plan to help Moses grow and develop into a leader worthy of the task he'd been assigned.

Rather than read through all of the details of each of the ten plagues (which many of you are familiar with), we will read select passages, focusing on Moses' journey to leadership and Pharaoh's rocky road to compliance. Both men resisted God's will. Each man witnessed God's glory. If you are not familiar with the story of the ten plagues, I encourage you to read through each account in its entirety. Glance at the chart on the next page. I've listed the passages describing each plague under the column labeled "Plague Name." To complete the table, simply read the verses listed under "Description & Passages to Read" and then fill in the "Person Acting" for each plague (I filled in some of the answers for you). Please also read the column labeled "Pharaoh's Response."

PLAGUE NAME	DESCRIPTION & VERSES TO READ	PERSON ACTING	PHARAOH'S RESPONSE
1 BLOOD Exodus 7:14–24	**Verses 19–23** *The water of the Nile was turned to blood.*	*Aaron*	*Pharaoh's wouldn't even listen and didn't take the events to heart.*
2 FROGS Exodus 8:1–15	**Verses 6–11,15** *Frogs invaded Egypt.*		*When Pharaoh saw there was relief, he hardened his heart and would not listen.*
3 GNATS Exodus 8:16–19	**Verses 17–19** *Dust in Egypt became gnats.*		*Magicians recognized this was "the finger of God," but Pharaoh's heart was hard.*
4 FLIES Exodus 8:20–32	**Verses 24–25,28-32** *Swarms of flies invaded Egypt.*	*The Lord*	*Pharaoh hardened his heart and would not let the Israelites go.*
5 LIVESTOCK Exodus 9:1–7	**Verses 5–7** *A terrible plague killed livestock.*	*The Lord*	*Pharaoh sent men to investigate, but his heart was unyielding.*
6 BOILS Exodus 9:8–12	**Verses 8–12** *Soot caused boils to breakout on people & animals.*		*The Lord hardened Pharaoh's heart, and he would not listen.*
7 HAIL Exodus 9:13–35	**Verses 23–28, 34–35** *A destructive hail storm fell on Egypt.*		*Pharaoh went back on his word. He and his officials hardened their hearts.*
8 LOCUSTS Exodus 10:1–20	**Verses 13–20** *Destructive locusts invaded Egypt.*		*Pharaoh admitted he sinned, but the Lord hardened his heart, and Pharaoh refused to let the Israelites go.*
9 DARKNESS Exodus 10:21-29	**Verses 21–28** *Total darkness covered Egypt for three days.*		*Pharaoh offered Moses a compromise and became angry when Moses refused. The Lord hardened Pharaoh's heart, and he refused to let Israel go.*

Before we discuss the final plague, let's analyze our data and make note of some additional information found within these passages.

Moses began Mission Deliverance as a fearful, reluctant man, simply obeying God's commands. But Moses was changed with each encounter of his dynamically present God. It was a different Moses who stretched out his hand toward the sky (Exodus 10:22), bringing the plague of darkness upon the Egyptians. A much bolder Moses confidently told Pharaoh, "You must allow us to have sacrifices and burnt offerings to present to the Lord our God" (Exodus 10:25). Moses was transformed by the glory of God.

God's Glory refers to a manifestation of God's active presence among His people, resulting in a greater revelation of His power and character.

Each plague was an expression of God's glory. Moses was changed by them. Pharaoh was not. Pharaoh began this plague-filled journey confident, uncooperative, and unimpressed with Moses or his God. Regardless how dynamic and existent Yahweh revealed Himself to be, the brash king refused to be changed by God's presence. He hardened his heart time and again. And by the sixth plague, God let Pharaoh have his way.

Each plague was an expression of God's glory. Moses was changed by them. Pharaoh was not.

Look back at the chart on page 55. Note the wording of Pharaoh's heart response during each of the following plagues:

1-Blood: ______________________

4-Flies: ______________________

5-Livestock: ______________________

6-Boils: ______________________

Pharaoh's heart was unyielding. He refused to accept that Yahweh was a living, dynamically present God. Despite how often our Lord chose to penetrate Pharaoh's world with miraculous expressions of His glorious presence, Pharaoh refused to acknowledge God's power and authority.

Pharaoh's heart was unyielding. He refused to accept that Yahweh was a living, dynamically present God.

According to Exodus 8:9–10, what reason did Moses give for allowing Pharaoh to set a time for the plague of frogs to end?

____

Pharaoh witnessed the glory of God. Yet, he dug in his heels and rejected the truth. God knew it would happen. He told Moses what to expect. Sadly, God gave Pharaoh over to his evil desires. He actually hardened Pharaoh's heart further to reveal His glory to the world.

Read Romans 1:22–25 and note the similarities in the people described in these passages and our hostile, unyielding, Egyptian king:

Moses and Pharaoh (as well as the king's officials) witnessed the glory of God. Each plague illuminated God's power and confirmed His existence. He invaded the Egyptian landscape with amazing manifestations of His active presence. Moses was strengthened, empowered and enlightened. Pharaoh willfully exchanged the undeniable truth of God for a lie. He refused to change. And now, God would bring about a plague so painful, so devastating, even the heard-hearted king would acknowledge the glory of Yahweh.

WEEK THREE DAY FOUR

Sleepless in Goshen

So Moses said, "This is what the Lord says: 'About midnight I will go throughout Egypt. There will be loud wailing throughout Egypt—worse than there has ever been or ever will be again.'"

EXODUS 11:4, 6

Yesterday we saw two different responses to the revelation of God's glory. Moses was strengthened by his encounters with a dynamically present God. Pharaoh was hardened by his encounters because God's plan didn't coincide with his agenda.

Look back at yesterday's lesson and write our definition of God's glory on the lines below:

Have you encountered God's glory? Have you been aware of His activity around you? Maybe He has comforted you or corrected you with a perfectly timed song on the radio. Or, perhaps He has answered your prayer through the loving, helpful hand of a neighbor. Share a time when you were aware of God's active presence in your life.

Have you encountered God's glory?

Nine plagues tormented Egypt, and their king stood firmly in the palace with his jaw set. Pharaoh refused to allow the Israelites to leave in order to worship their God. In order to set the stage for the tenth and final plague, please re-read the entire account of the thick, eerie ninth plague of darkness that descended upon Egypt for three days.

Read Exodus 10:21–29.

What distinction did God make between the Egyptians and Israelites during the ninth plague?

Egypt was in ruins. Their crops had been destroyed by hail and locusts. Their livestock were dead. The usually vibrant country was brought to a gloomy halt, as it was eclipsed by a darkness so intense it could "be felt" by everyone in Egypt. The people became visionless prisoners in their homes for three days. In contrast, Goshen escaped the lurking darkness and continued on with life as usual. Pharaoh summoned Moses to the dark Egyptian palace. Once there, Moses was again offered an unacceptable compromise. Pharaoh tried to ensure his free workforce would return (or at least guarantee the Hebrew livestock would replace some of the devastating loss his country had endured). But Pharaoh wasn't in any position to negotiate, and Moses was determined to

Egypt was in ruins.

follow God's instructions to the letter. "Not a hoof" was to remain in Egypt.

How did Pharaoh respond to Moses' insistence on taking the livestock?

Backed into a corner, Pharaoh ordered Moses to get out of his sight and threatened to kill him the next time he saw his face. As the hard-hearted king uttered those murderous threats, his last opportunity to avoid God's wrath passed.

Read Exodus 11:1–3. What did God tell Moses prior to this last meeting with Pharaoh?

What impact had the plagues had on the Egyptian people's opinion of Moses?

Now read Moses' parting comments to Pharaoh in Exodus 11:4–10.

The tables had turned. Moses angrily told Pharaoh exactly what would happen next. The Egyptians may have bowed before the once revered king and cowered at his commands, but as the first born in Egypt breathed their last breaths, the Egyptians would fall, grief stricken before Moses and beg the Israelites to leave.

These are agonizing passages to read, and this is a tough lesson for me to write. It's easy to focus upon the merciful, compassionate nature of our Lord and forget He is also a powerful God who expects obedience. Obedience is the theme of our lesson today. It was crucial the Israelites carried out each detail of God's plan carefully in order for their families to exit Egypt alive.

These are agonizing passages to read, and this is a tough lesson for me to write.

Read Exodus 12:1–13.

What was each man told to do on the tenth day of the month, and what was to be done four days later (vv. 3 and 6)?

How strange God's instructions must have seemed to the Israelites. They hadn't ever prepared a meal like this one. Each family had to select a year-old lamb and then care for it for four days. Can you imagine how attached the children must have become (adults too!) to those little lambs? Over the years, my children have begged to keep every stray dog that has wandered onto the Ferguson lawn. When Mark and I let Brandon and Brianna feed and take care of an animal for even a single day, they had it named and were arguing over where it was going to sleep. I would guess slaughtering that lamb and roasting its meat for dinner after caring for it for four days must have been traumatic for these families.

How strange God's instructions must have seemed to the Israelites.

But God had a specific purpose for His odd set of instructions and even before it all happened, He made it clear this meal had tremendous significance. It was unlike any meal they had ever eaten. It was "the Lord's Passover."

Read Exodus 12:21–23.

What were they to do with the lamb's blood according to verse 22?

____

____

The Israelites had never slaughtered a lamb and drained its blood into a basin. They'd never grabbed a handful of hyssop and dipped it like a paint brush into the blood, applying it to their door frames.

According to verse 23, what was the purpose of applying the blood on the door frames?

____

____

Read Exodus 12:24–28. How did the Israelites respond to God's plan?

____

Picture yourself in one of these Hebrew homes. What thoughts might be going through your mind as you set out to follow God's instructions carefully, knowing your child's life depended upon your strict adherence to the plan? How would you respond to your children's concerns over slaughtering "their" lamb and their questions about the blood on the doorframe?

Whatever your answer, one thing is clear: God said to do this and His people obeyed. The requests may have seemed strange. The act was, perhaps, frightening to the children and unsettling to the parents. But God's people had faith He was about to once again penetrate their world with a powerful manifestation of His active presence. They fearfully obeyed His instructions to the letter.

The families gathered to eat that night ready to leave. They had their sandals on, and their cloaks were tucked into their belts. Dads held their roasted lamb in one hand and gripped their staffs with the other. As midnight approached, an eerie silence must have descended upon each house. I imagine children peered curiously at their parents, watching for indications all would be okay in their blood-covered homes. And then . . . it happened. God kept his Word.

> We may not always like what God says, but we can always count on Him to keep His Word.

Read Exodus 12:29–30.

Midnight ushered in the fulfillment of all God had been telling Moses since his life-changing encounter at the burning bush in Midian. We may not always like what God says, but we can always count on Him to keep His Word. Moses struggled with confidence and wrestled with doubt, but he ultimately obeyed God's commands, and he urged the Israelites to do the same.

What does 1 Samuel 15:22 tell you about God's perspective on obedience?

The Israelites obeyed. They slaughtered their lambs, painted their door frames with blood, and ate their last meal on Egyptian soil "in haste," anxiously awaiting the freedom they had been promised. Their obedience was evidence of their faith that their God would indeed keep His word on what must have been a sleepless night in Goshen.

WEEK THREE | **DAY FIVE**

Personal Application

In Day One of this week's lesson, we saw Moses discouraged even though God clearly told him Pharaoh would refuse to allow the Israelites to leave Egypt. In Day Two, we observed God relaying His plan to reveal Himself to the Israelites as Yahweh—their dynamically present covenant keeper. Then, we discovered in Day Three's lesson that God's glory refers to a manifestation of His active presence among His people, resulting in a greater revelation of His power and character. And finally in Day Four, the final plague descended upon Egypt, as every firstborn among them died during the night. Only by the blood of the Passover lamb was an Israelite home covered and their firstborn spared.

How is Jesus described in 1 Corinthians 5:7? ______________________________

Rather than the usual format, for this week's personal application lesson, I'd like to reflect upon the greatest manifestation of God's active presence among His people—the ultimate revelation of God's glory—when our Lord chose to invade our world as the person of Jesus Christ, our Passover Lamb.

Re-read Exodus 12:3–9 and fill in the requested information about a Passover lamb.

Each family chose a lamb without ______________________ (v. 5)

The lamb was slaughtered on the fourteenth day of the month at what time of day? ______________________. (v. 6)

Families were to take some of the blood and put it on the ______________________

and ______________________ of their doorframes. (v. 7)

Rather than boiling the lamb, it was ______________ over a fire. (v. 9)

According to Exodus 12:46, how were the Israelites to handle the slaughtered lamb's bones?

____

Every detail for preparing a Passover lamb was carefully relayed to the Israelites, and they cautiously followed God's meticulous instructions. Lives were at stake. God's punishment was descending upon Egypt and only the blood of the Passover lamb could protect the Israelites' firstborn sons.

Every detail for preparing a Passover lamb was carefully relayed to the Israelites, and they cautiously followed God's meticulous instructions.

But there was an even greater significance to the details God outlined for the Passover preparations. Those lambs foreshadowed the sacrifice Jesus made as He allowed Himself to be slain on the cross to save us from the punishment for our sins.

Let's examine each detail you have noted on page 62 to determine if Jesus met the requirements of a Passover Lamb.

The lamb had to be blemish free—a flawless sacrifice. Read the following passages and note what you learn about the condition of Jesus.

Hebrews 4:14–15:

---

1 Peter 1:18–19:

The Passover lamb was slaughtered at twilight, which was between 3 and 5 PM.[15] According to Matthew 27:45–50, at approximately what time did Jesus give up His spirit? ***(Note: The sixth hour is noon.)***

Israelite families were instructed to take blood from their Passover lamb and place it on the tops and sides of their door frames. As Jesus hung on the cross, a crown of thorns pierced His head, and nails were driven through His hands and feet. How might the blood on the doorframes of the Israelites' homes have foreshadowed the blood stained cross upon which Jesus died?

Exodus 12:46 tells us no bones of the Passover lamb were to be broken. Read John 19:33–37 and note what you learn about the fulfillment of these verses?

Once the lamb was slaughtered and prepared for cooking, rather than boiling the lamb meat, which was the usual cooking method, God instructed the Israelites to roast the Passover lamb over a fire. If you are like me, you are wondering why God was so specific about the manner in which the lamb was cooked. Interestingly, I found a fascinating quote from Justin Martyr, a respected philosopher who lived about a hundred years after Jesus was crucified and was martyred for his faith:

> "For the lamb, which is roasted, is roasted and dressed up in the form of the cross. For one spit is transfixed right through from the lower parts up to the head, and one across the back, to which are attached the legs of the lamb."[16]

According to Martyr, a Passover lamb was roasted over a fire in the shape of a cross. Isn't that amazing? The Israelites simply obeyed God's instructions. They couldn't possibly have understood the significance of roasting their Passover lamb on a wooden cross. But we now know Jesus is our Passover Lamb. Every detail of the Passover meal that saved the Israelites' first-born sons and brought about their deliverance that fateful night in Egypt foreshadowed God's ultimate plan to deliver all nations (Genesis 12:3) through the sacrifice of His Son, Jesus.

Our Lord demonstrated His unfailing love for us as Jesus died upon the cross. Read Romans 6:23 below and underline what we earned because of our sinful behavior:

For the wages of sin is death, but the gift of God is eternal life in Christ Jesus our Lord (NIV 84).

Through faith in Jesus, our Passover Lamb, we have in essence been covered by the blood of the Lamb. God chooses to pass over us, withholding the punishment we rightfully deserve and granting us, instead, the precious gift of eternal life.

Through faith in Jesus, our Passover Lamb, we have in essence been covered by the blood of the Lamb.

As a way of closing, read Revelation 5:11 – 13 and note heaven's response to the sacrifice of our Passover Lamb.

End today by writing your own words of praise on the lines below. "Worthy is the Lamb who was slain, to receive . . . honor and glory and praise!"

Week 4

Beyond Egypt

WEEK FOUR DAY ONE

The Other Side of Glory

When Pharaoh stubbornly refused to let us go, the Lord killed every firstborn in Egypt, both man and animal. This is why I sacrifice to the Lord the first male offspring of every womb and redeem each of my firstborn sons.

EXODUS 13:15

Begin today by writing our definition for God's glory on the lines below (If you need help, look back at page 56).

God is active and present in our world on a daily basis. His glory is revealed when He chooses to make us aware of His active presence around us. Encounters with God's glory are usually positive, encouraging, and empowering experiences. However, today we will look at the other side of glory. Sometimes, our encounters with God's glory not only yield a renewed sense of awe or respect, they also incite a healthy measure of fear.

Begin today by reading Exodus 12:12–13 and 29–36.

Pharaoh's own firstborn son was dead. Before the night was over, he summoned for Moses and Aaron. He didn't just grant their request to leave for a few days, the humbled king ordered Moses and his people to take their livestock and get out of Egypt for good.

Pharaoh's kingdom had endured pests, treacherous hail, painful boils, and the devastating loss of their livestock. They had been prisoners of a dreadful darkness for three days and three nights. But the loss of their children was more than even the relentless king could withstand.

Several years ago, the two-year old son of a woman attending our church died after falling from the second-story window of her home during a family gathering. Our entire church was shaken by grief. I will never forget the image of the tiny white coffin containing the body of the black-haired, pudgy little boy. Just a week earlier, the adorable toddler had been skipping through the halls of our church preschool, grasping his mamma's hand. At the funeral, the young mother could hardly support her own weight when she attempted to stand and hug my neck. Her pain affected me deeply. I was overcome with sadness and wrestled with a sense of indignation over the death of such an innocent young life. I was brought to my knees with grief at the sight of that family's pain.

Have you ever known someone who experienced the death of a child? Maybe you've lost a child yourself. If so, words cannot express how sorry I am for the loss you endured. If you can find the words, describe how that event impacted you.

I don't believe for a moment that Moses was unaffected by the horrific scene in Egypt. He heard the heart-rending wails of grief-stricken parents. He looked into the pain-riddled eyes of Pharaoh. I imagine Moses wrestled with indignation over those children's deaths, just as we would. He probably left the palace that day with a profound respect for the mighty power of his Lord.

And Pharaoh? This time, he didn't scoff at Moses' dynamically present God. The Lord's wrath had been released upon the king's kingdom and not even the royal firstborn was exempt. What surprising request did Pharaoh make of Moses at the end of Exodus 12:32?

The heart-broken ruler acknowledged his vulnerability by requesting a blessing. Pharaoh had also gained respect for Yahweh. The Lord said He would punish the nation His people served as slaves, and Moses had relayed the message to Pharaoh (Exodus 4:23). Yahweh is a promise keeper. We may not always like what He says, but we can count on Him to keep His Word. The Israelites were learning that truth . . . and so were the Egyptians.

Yahweh is a promise keeper.

What request did the Israelites make of the Egyptians in Exodus 12:35?

According to Exodus 3:22, who did the asking?

While the Israelite men spent their days doing slave labor, the women had cared for their children and their homes. They knew their neighbors, Hebrew and Egyptian alike. I can't imagine how difficult it was for the Israelite women to ask their grieving Egyptian neighbors for jewelry and clothing. But with the frightening display of God's glory still fresh on their minds, the Hebrew women asked, and Egyptian women quickly responded. The Israelites indeed plundered the Egyptians, just as the Lord said they would.

Let's see what happened as the Israelites moved beyond their astounding encounter with God's glory that dreadful night in Egypt. Please read Exodus 12:37–51.

As God's people left Egypt, they were instructed to remember what the Lord had done.

What interesting fact is shared in Exodus 12:38?

Let me just say, I'm not very comfortable with the content of Exodus 12. I don't like the idea of God killing innocent children as punishment for the actions of their obstinate king.

Writing this lesson has been difficult and uncomfortable . . . and troubling. But as much as I want to focus upon positive displays of God's glory, such as times when He heals a terminally ill patient or mercifully redeems a rebellious, drug addicted teenager, the fact is, this world contains a multitude of people who have absolutely no fear of God and sometimes a frightening encounter with the other side of glory is the only way to get their attention.

The fact is, this world contains a multitude of people who have absolutely no fear of God and sometimes a frightening encounter with the other side of glory is the only way to get their attention.

The Pharaoh (and probably the entire Egyptian population) had no fear of Yahweh; no respect or concern for His power and position as Creator. Pharaoh scoffed when Moses asked him to allow the Hebrew slaves to go and worship their Lord. It wasn't until Pharaoh witnessed the final, devastating tenth plague that he complied with Yahweh's request. Sometimes, hearts are only moved by a frightening display of God's glory.

After that heart-rending night in Egypt, it appears many people developed respect for Yahweh; so much so, they opted to follow Him and leave the country along with the Israelites. We might like to forget the events that occurred in the wee hours of the night during the Exodus, but the Lord felt they were so profoundly important, He commanded His people to commemorate that night for generations to come.

Read Exodus 13:1–16.

The people gathered at Succoth before heading into the vast desert, and Moses relayed the importance of the events they had just witnessed. The lumps of yeast-less dough the women had packed away in clothing would become a lasting memory, rekindled each year when they celebrated the feast of Unleavened Bread. God's people would always remember this night when God brought them out of Egypt, sparing their firstborn sons by the blood of the lamb. From that day forward, all firstborn among the Israelites belonged to God. They were to commemorate this night by sacrificing the firstborn of all of their livestock and redeeming their firstborn sons with five shekels (Numbers 18:16) to buy them back from God's service.

According to Exodus 13:16, what was the reason God wanted His people to do these rituals?

Encounters with God's glory should impact us for the rest of our lives. Whether frightening or comforting, after experiencing a manifestation of God's active presence, our dedication should be more evident, our worship richer, and our hearts more tender.

Encounters with God's glory should impact us for the rest of our lives.

According to Hebrews 11:27, what was the reason Moses persevered and led God's people out of Egypt?

Moses was an eyewitness to God's glory. He didn't just believe Yahweh existed and cared about His people; Moses knew it by experience. That knowledge gave him the courage to persevere. Likewise, our lives should be inherently different on the other side of glory.

WEEK FOUR | DAY TWO

Glory at the Sea

The waters were divided, and the Israelites went through the sea on dry ground, with a wall of water on their right and on their left.

EXODUS 14:21-22

One of the best birthday presents I ever received was a GPS, which, by the way, stands for Global Positioning System. My husband, Mark, gave me the thoughtful gift because I had gotten lost a few times while traveling by myself. My favorite feature on the device is the "Home" button. I take great comfort knowing regardless how far I venture from my house in Cypress, Texas, I can select "Home" and the GPS will always lead me the most direct route back to my home.

As the Israelites exited Egypt for their Promised Land, it is probably a good thing Global Positioning Systems had not yet been invented. Moses did not take God's people the shortest route west to their new home. Instead, he led them south into the desert, toward the Red Sea.

As the Israelites exited Egypt for their Promised Land, it is probably a good thing Global Positioning Systems had not yet been invented.

Read Exodus 13:17–22.

According to verse 17, who led the people away from the road to the Promised Land?

What was the reason for sending them an indirect route (v. 17)?

Interestingly, how does verse 18 describe the Israelites as they went up out of Egypt?

Isn't it comforting to know God is aware of our weaknesses even when we are not? At the time of the Exodus, the path through Philistine territory was a military road for the Egyptians.[17] God knew His people weren't mentally, or perhaps physically, ready for a military confrontation. The Israelites enthusiastically marched out of Egypt, armed for battle, but God knew their zeal was misplaced. A confrontation would send those former Hebrew slaves running right back to the "iron-smelting furnace." God protected the overconfident soldiers by sending them into the desert.

Isn't it comforting to know God is aware of our weaknesses even when we are not?

What confirmation did the Israelites have that it was God who was guiding them along their journey (vv. 21–22)?

The Israelites had lived in Egypt for 430 years. By comparison, America was formed as a nation less than 300 years ago. The Israelites who marched out of Egypt that day were just as entrenched in the Egyptian culture as most of us are rooted in the American way of life. At least four generations of Israelites had been born and raised in Egypt. The homes they left in haste were all they had ever known. Leaving Egypt was risky and probably a bit frightening. It must have brought them great comfort to see the massive pillar of cloud gracing the landscape ahead of them. God was with them. And as the sun slipped below the western horizon, the billowy pillar miraculously transformed into a blazing column of fire. Much was uncertain, but they had the assurance that God was leading them and lighting their path through the desert.

How I have longed for a pillar of cloud to guide me along my spiritual journey—or at least a Spiritual Positioning System to tell me when I need to take a detour in order to avoid a confrontation for which I am unprepared. I've sometimes wished for a pillar of fire to light my way back after becoming distracted from my pursuit of God's path.

What about you? Are you confident you are where God has directed you at the moment? If you could see the pillar of cloud, do you think it would be right before you or have you wondered away from God's path, distracted by the demands and treasures of our culture? Would your Spiritual Positioning System tell you to "make a U-turn" or do you think you would hear "continue" in the direction you are heading?

What about you? Are you confident you are where God has directed you at the moment?

As we return to the scene along the sea, God's people appear to be "wandering around the land in confusion," but God's divine pillar is leading them each step of the way. Please read Exodus 14:1–12.

How do these passages confirm God's words, "If they face war, they might change their minds and return to Egypt"?

God made sure the Israelites did not have the option of returning to slavery. They were trapped in the desert with their backs to the sea. Faced with the impressive Egyptian army comprised of more than six hundred chariots, officers, horsemen, and their troops, the ill-equipped soldiers forgot all about the majestic pillar of cloud (which was still there, by the way). They were terrified with nowhere to run.

Read Exodus 14:13–18.

Hasn't Moses grown? "Stand firm and you will see the deliverance the Lord will bring you today." Those faith-filled words were uttered by the same man who begged God to send someone else to deliver His people out of Egypt.

Record Moses' words from Exodus 14:14 below:

Did you need to read those words today? What battles or Red Sea-type obstacles are you facing right now? Read Moses' words to the Israelites again. Do you believe them? The Lord will fight for you. That's the lesson the Israelites were about to learn as they stood, hemmed in with the Egyptians charging toward them.

Read Exodus 14:19–31 slowly and try to picture the events as you read.

The Lord indeed fought for His people. Look back at Exodus 14:17. What did God say was His purpose for the miraculous display of His active presence at the Red Sea?

Write our definition for God's glory again on the lines below (Look back at page 56 if you need help):

God doesn't reveal His glory simply to show off. He wanted the Israelites and the Egyptians to recognize His active presence among them. What do the following passages indicate happened as a result of God's actions at the Red Sea?

God doesn't reveal His glory simply to show off. He wanted the Israelites and the Egyptians to recognize His active presence among them.

Exodus 14:18: ______________________________

____

Exodus 14:25: ______________________________

____

Exodus 14:31: ______________________________

____

God's glory displayed at the Sea indeed resulted in a greater revelation of His power and character—for the Israelites as well as the Egyptians. God's people feared Him and trusted Moses as His servant. The Egyptian soldiers recognized Yahweh was the One fighting against them, and by the end of the night, there was no doubt in their minds they were on the wrong side of that miraculous pillar of fire. The Egyptians who chose to follow God and leave Egypt with the Israelites acknowledged Yahweh as the true Lord.

Read Exodus 15:4–5, 19–21, which includes a portion of the praise song God's people sang as they celebrated this amazing display of God's glory at the Red Sea.

Have you ever written a song? As a way of closing our lesson today, write a short song to your Lord. You don't have to be an experienced singer to write a heartfelt jingle. Has God proven His faithfulness to you recently? Has there been a time when you were aware of God's active presence around you? Using the Israelites' song as an example, write a short song about your experience. If you need a tune, write your own words to a familiar chorus or children's song. Have fun with it. If you dare, share your song with your small group.

____

____

____

WEEK FOUR DAY THREE

Uncertainty in the Desert of Shur

There the Lord made a decree and a law for them, and there He tested them.

EXODUS 15:25B

We last saw the Israelites celebrating and singing God's praises on the shore of the Red Sea. Miriam, Moses and Aaron's sister, grabbed a tambourine and led the women in what must have resembled a modern-day Conga line, as they danced and sang a jubilant song to the Lord. The Israelites were elated. God had delivered them with a miraculous display of His glory at the sea.

Begin today by reading Exodus 15:22–26.

According to verse 24, what were the people concerned about as they grumbled against Moses?

No one was dancing or shaking tambourines three days later when the newly freed slaves hadn't encountered a single source of drinkable water in the Desert of Shur. Reflect for a moment on traveling experiences with your family. How did relational challenges increase as comfort levels decreased?

No one was dancing or shaking tambourines three days later when the newly freed slaves hadn't encountered a single source of drinkable water in the Desert of Shur.

I picture the Israelite children whiny and their parents grumpy. I imagine elderly folks complained about their aches and pains. Throats were parched, and eyes were gritty. The irritable, weary travelers looked around and the only water in sight was the brackish, bitter water of Marah. The homeless crowds were losing hope, as the provision of their basic needs seemed ***unsure*** in the rugged wilderness of the Desert of Shur.

Mark and I recently had a Desert of Shur experience when he was laid off from his job. At first, we were confident he would find a new position quickly. However, after three long months of diligently searching and posting for open positions, Mark had gone on two interviews that hadn't panned out and all of his other leads had dried up. As the weeks passed, our savings dwindled, despite our efforts to trim expenses. There were days when we stood strong in our faith, certain God would provide, just as He has always done. But there were also days when our faith waned and we began to lose hope that he would ever find a new job in his field. To make matters worse, our daughter was entering her first year of college, and the weight of our responsibilities was heavy upon our hearts. The days seemed long and, at times, God's provision appeared unsure in our Desert of Shur.

Have you ever spent some time in a Desert of Shur? If so, what need did you fear might not be met?

____

____

What did God tell Moses to do in order to meet the people's need for drinkable water (v. 25)?

____

According to verse 25, why did God allow His people to go days without a basic need in the Desert of Shur?

____

God allows Desert of Shur experiences to test us. Thankfully, we can rest assured He knows just how long we are able to endure desert tests. When His people were indeed desperate for life-sustaining liquid, the Lord told Moses to throw a piece of wood into the bitter water, and it instantly became sweet.

> God allows Desert of Shur experiences to test us.

The crowds drank and were refreshed. God then told His people what He expected during their desert travels and, if they listened and obeyed, He promised He wouldn't bring the diseases upon them that He brought upon the Egyptians (a thought that had probably crossed some of their minds).

God's people knew Him as God Almighty (***El Shaddai***)—an all-sufficient, all-powerful God. They were in the process of learning to know Him as the Lord (***Yahweh***)—their dynamically present promise keeper. Then suddenly, in the middle of their Desert of Shur, just after making the waters of Marah sweet, God presented another of His attributes by introducing Himself by a new name.

How does God describe himself at the end of Exodus 15:26?

In Hebrew, this name is listed as ***Yahweh Rapha*** (usually translated ***Jehovah Rapha***)—the God who heals. ***Rapha*** means, "to heal, make healthful, to heal (of God); figuratively it can mean to heal water or pottery, national hurts or individual distresses.[18]

God provided a vivid illustration for His people. He wanted them to know that just as He healed the bitter water of Marah, He was able to heal their hurts as a nation and restore them. Yes, He is able to bring devastating plagues, as He did in Egypt, but God is also the only source of true wellness. He can make a broken heart whole again. His presence is like soothing ointment upon our deepest wounds. He is able to heal the sick and to provide a disillusioned soul in the middle of the bitterest of circumstances, with life-sustaining hope and refreshment. He is ***Jehovah Rapha***, the Lord, who heals you.

Whether God healed emotional wounds of your past, restored your hope when you thought all hope was gone, or brought you through a life-threatening illness, share how you have experienced God as ***Jehovah Rapha***.

Read Exodus 15:27. What was significant about the place ***Jehovah Rapha*** took His people to rest and recover from the Desert of Shur?

After a time of testing in a Desert of Shur, God is faithful to provide rest and refreshment. That's what we need after enduring a time of uncertainty and scarcity. God provided rest for His people in Elim. They drank all the water they needed from twelve fresh water springs and lounged in the shade of seventy lush palm trees.

After a time of testing in a Desert of Shur, God is faithful to provide rest and refreshment.

My dear sister in Christ, if you have recently spent some time in a Desert of Shur, you can look forward to an Elim in your future. ***Jehovah Rapha*** is the God who heals you. He knows just what you need to be restored and refreshed after a long desert journey.

WEEK FOUR DAY FOUR

Unprecedented Provision

That evening quail came and covered the camp, and in the morning there was a layer of dew around the camp.

EXODUS 16:13

The Israelites' rested in Elim and enjoyed a reprieve from the dry, desert wilderness between Egypt and their promised land. They relaxed, enjoyed their families, perhaps even took a few swims in the cool spring waters of God's provision. The intense journey through the Desert of Shur was a distant memory and life was good. However, there was a lot of territory yet to cover and God's people needed to move on.

Now read Exodus 16:1–3.

According to verse 1, when did the Israelites leave Elim and enter the Desert of Sin?

God's people had soaked up the abundance of Elim for a couple months. However, as the homeless travelers encountered yet another desert, it didn't take long for them to start grumbling all over again.

Who did the Israelites blame for their circumstances (v. 2)?

Now read Exodus 16:4–9.

Look back at verses 8 and 9. What did Moses want the people to understand?

The same God who delivered them from Egypt, parted the Red Sea, and provided rest at Elim, is the same God who allowed the Israelites to suffer in the desert. They weren't complaining about anything Moses had done. The former-shepherd-turned-leader was simply following God's instructions. The Israelites were grumbling against God.

The same God who delivered them from Egypt, parted the Red Sea, and provided rest at Elim, is the same God who allowed the Israelites to suffer in the desert.

Let's take a moment to observe the attitude of a man who endured far more hardship than extreme thirst and prolonged hunger. As a matter of fact, Job experienced more heartache and pain than most of us will ever endure, and yet, after receiving the news of loss after heart-rending loss, Job chose to worship God instead of grumble against Him.

Please read Job 1:6–22.

How is Job described in verse 8?

Summarize what happened to Job:

If we are willing to accept times in Elim, we must also be willing to humbly receive the hardship and pain of a desert. God indeed gives, but He sometimes takes away. In the words of Job, "Shall we accept good from God, and not trouble?" (Job 2:10). Will we choose to worship Him through both? If not, we could find ourselves shaking our fists at God, grumbling against Him, and succumbing to bitterness. If instead, we choose to worship Him, our God can even bring sweetness to a tumultuous trek through the most barren of deserts.

God indeed gives, but He sometimes takes away.

The Israelites grumbled and complained, reminiscing about their days in Egypt when they "sat around pots of meat and ate all the food they wanted" (Exodus 16:3). Let's take a moment for a reality check. Read Exodus 2:11, 23; 4:31. Describe the Israelites' circumstances back in good ol' Egypt:

Before you are too hard on this ungrateful bunch, let's pause for a reality check of our own. Look back at your own words as you shared how you have experienced God as Jehovah Rapha (page 78). Now, consider how often you complain or long for days past, despite God's glorious work in your life. How do you, at times, resemble the Israelites?

I would guess we all can act a bit unappreciative at times and have done our share of complaining. Let's see how God responded to the Israelites' ungrateful grumbling in the desert.

> I would guess we all can act a bit unappreciative at times and have done our share of complaining.

Please read Exodus 16:8–15.

Sadly, God's people were so focused upon their discomfort, they were no longer enamored with the billowy expression of God's active presence that had been leading them through the desert during their entire journey. God delivered them from slavery, parted the Red Sea, destroyed the enemy who pursued them, turned bitter water sweet, provided rest and refreshment in Elim . . . and yet, as soon as they became uncomfortable, His people once again grumbled and complained.

With Moses' words, "You are not grumbling against us, but against the Lord" fresh on their minds (and, hopefully, their hearts), Aaron told the people the Lord had been listening and they were to gather before Him. I don't know about you, but I would have been trembling in my sandals as I stood in that hot desert sand.

What appeared in the familiar pillar of cloud (v. 10)? ____________________

The people had grown accustomed to seeing the miraculous pillar of cloud leading their way through the desert. But something distinctive happened. Perhaps the cloud brightened or the top darkened. Scripture doesn't tell us exactly what changed about the billowy pillar, but as the people of God stood looking toward the desert, the entire Israelite community received a fresh awareness of His active presence among them. And what aspect of God's character did they encounter? His mercy.

How did God respond (vv. 13–15)?

____

____

____

____

____

God responded to His people's ungrateful complaining by supplying the meat they desired and the daily bread they required. That, my sister in Christ, is abundant, undeserved, glorious mercy.

Read Psalm 103:8–14. What more do you learn about the merciful, compassionate nature of our God?

A massive flock of quail descended upon the Desert of Sin that evening, just as God said it would. I'm sure it wasn't long before the Israelite campsite was filled with the aroma of meat roasting over an open fire. With full bellies, the weary travelers probably slept well that night and were awakened to an extraordinary layer of dew all around the camp. When the dew melted, mysterious thin flakes of God's merciful provision appeared on the desert floor.

God is compassionate and gracious, slow to anger and abounding in love (Psalm 103:8).

God is compassionate and gracious, slow to anger and abounding in love (Psalm 103:8). Thankfully, He remembers how we were formed and knows we are mere dust. As God listened to His people's ungrateful grumbling in the Desert of Sin, He chose to respond with an unprecedented display of His glorious provision. He truly does not treat His people as our sins deserve.

WEEK FOUR | DAY FIVE

Personal Application

Application for Day One:

As God unleashed the Plague of the First Born on Egypt, Israelite and Egyptian alike saw a manifestation of God's active presence unlike any they had seen before. There indeed was a "loud wailing throughout Egypt" (Exodus 11:6). The Egyptians urged the Israelites to leave, and God's people gathered up their families, wrapped up their yeast-free dough, and hot-footed it toward the border.

To refresh your memory, who went with the Israelites, according to Exodus 12:38?

The other people included Egyptians and, perhaps, slaves native to other countries.[19] The escalating plagues convinced everyone in Egypt that the God of the Israelites was the true God. There was no doubt He was active and present . . . and powerful. The Pharaoh they had feared for years was no match for Yahweh and as the Exodus began, many (not just a few) other people followed God's chosen leader out of Egypt.

> As believers in Christ, we have the privilege of making people aware of God's active presence by the way we live our lives.

When God's glory is revealed, people respond. As believers in Christ, we have the privilege of making people aware of God's active presence by the way we live our lives. Read the following passages, and note what you learn about some of the ways in which we glorify God:

Matthew 5:14–16: ______________________________

____

1 Corinthians 10:31—11:1: ____________________

____

In essence, as believers in Christ, we have the Holy Spirit of our Lord living within us, empowering us to live in a manner that reflects the goodness of the Lord we serve. When we yield to His Spirit and choose to live in accordance with His Word, the world around us experiences the evidence of God's active presence at work within us. It's like taking a giant magnifying glass and positioning it so others can see Christ in us.

Application for Day Two

After letting the Israelites leave Egypt, Pharaoh and his officials suddenly realized they had let their free workforce leave the country. The determined king immediately summoned over six hundred chariots and officers from his army. They charged into the desert after the Israelites, who were trapped with the Red Sea behind them.

According to Exodus 14:10–12, how did the Israelites react when they saw the Egyptian army?

____

God told Moses to raise his staff over the sea. When he did, the waters miraculously parted and the Israelites crossed the sea on dry ground, saving them from their enemy.

Read Exodus 14:31. How did God's people respond to His miraculous display of His glory at the Red Sea?

____

Now read Psalm 20:1–9. If a friend was facing what seemed to be an insurmountable obstacle, how might you encourage her by relaying the story of the parting of the Red Sea and the prayer contained in Psalm 20?

____

____

____

When you share how God has responded in the past and relay how God is working in the present, you are glorifying God by drawing someone's attention to His active presence, you are highlighting His power and character. When God is glorified, people find the courage to trust Him, even in the midst of their modern-day Red Sea trials.

Application for Day Three

The Israelites traveled through the Desert of Shur for three days without finding water. They were grumpy and exhausted. When they arrived at Marah and encountered only bitter, undrinkable water, their frustration escalated, and they grumbled against Moses, blaming him for their dire circumstances. When Moses cried out to God on the Israelites' behalf, God showed him a piece of wood. Moses then tossed it into the bitter water, and it instantly became sweet, drinkable water.

Now read Matthew 6:25–34. What examples did Jesus use to reassure us that God will meet our basic needs?

What did Jesus tell us to seek after rather than worrying about our physical needs?

Trusting God when our circumstances appear hopeless is far easier to think about than to carry out. When Mark was without work for over three months without a single viable job lead, I knew I needed to trust God to meet our basic needs. I knew God is faithful (still do!) and worthy of our trust. I could recite Matthew 6:33 from memory (and did). But one day when things looked bleakest, I woke up in the wee hours of the morning in a state of panic. I spent hours on my knees with my face planted in living room carpet, pausing to run to the bathroom to throw-up between prayers. I was captivated by fear and worry. It took two days for me to wrestle with my fear and come back to a place of peace and rest in God's presence. Even then, I had to keep God's Word and examples of His past faithfulness ever before me to keep the fear from overtaking me again.

Trusting God when our circumstances appear hopeless is far easier to think about than to carry out.

You can trust God to meet your basic needs. Just as He responded to Moses' cries for help, He will respond to your prayers. He is faithful. He is indeed worthy of our trust. He may not always respond as quickly as we would like or in the specific way we expect, but just as God provides for the birds and has crafted the beauty of Lilies in a field, He is able to provide for you (see Matthew 6:26–28). Just as He turned the bitter waters of Marah sweet with Moses' simple act of obedience in the Desert of Shur, God is able to supply all of your needs as you seek Him and do your best to walk in His ways.

Application for Day Four

Despite all God had done for His people, they grumbled and complained as they traveled through the Desert of Sin.

Read the following passage and underline the actions we should take when we find ourselves in need.

Do not be anxious about anything, but in everything, by prayer and petition, with thanksgiving, present your requests to God. Finally, brothers, whatever is true, whatever is noble, whatever is right, whatever is pure, whatever is lovely, whatever is admirable—if anything is excellent or praiseworthy—think about such things. (Philippians 4:6, 8; NIV '84)

Read Hebrews 5:7–9 and note what Jesus learned through His suffering:

____

____

> When we find ourselves in need, rather than complaining and grumbling as the Israelites did, we need to pray with sincere gratitude for the things we do have.

When we find ourselves in need, rather than complaining and grumbling as the Israelites did, we need to pray with sincere gratitude for the things we do have, crying out to God for help, with an attitude of submission toward His sovereign will and purposes. You may feel your complaints are justified and your needs are vast. Like me when Mark was out of work, you may feel frightened as you encounter hardships or trials, but before you allow bitterness to take root in your heart, voice your concerns honestly before God. You may have to spend a few tearful hours with your face planted in the carpet, but just be honest and real with your Lord. He knows what you need, and He is somehow at work in your trials. Even Jesus offered up prayers and petitions with loud cries and tears. Even Jesus learned obedience through suffering.

Read James 1:2–4. What else do you learn about the purpose God may have for allowing you to endure seasons of trial or hardship?

God just may be refining you and perfecting you through suffering. He wants you to become "mature and complete, not lacking anything" (James 1:4). If he allowed His Son to suffer to accomplish His will, we should not expect anything less.

Consider it pure joy, my [sisters], whenever you face trials of many kinds, because you know that the testing of your faith develops perseverance. Perseverance must finish its work so that you may be mature and complete, not lacking anything. (James 1:2–4)

Week Five

Desert Rumblings

WEEK FIVE DAY ONE

Desert Provisions

When the Israelites saw it, they said to each other, "What is it?"
For they did not know what it was.

EXODUS 16:15

As I am writing this lesson today, the sun is shining for the first time after several days of storms and flooding near our home in Cypress, Texas. The backyard is still soggy, but the grass and plants are dark shades of lush green. After being cooped up indoors, I enjoyed walking the dog earlier today with the hot summer sun shining on my face.

When we last closed our workbooks, the Israelites were probably doing anything they could think of to shelter their skin from the intense sun. There was no rain in their forecast. As they scanned the horizon, they saw nothing but dry, dusty sand and an occasional pale desert bush. They were grumpy and dissatisfied in the Desert of Sin, but God mercifully responded by providing quail in the evening and mysterious bread from heaven in the morning.

According to Exodus 16:15, how did the Israelites respond to the site of the strange, thin flakes covering the desert floor?

This heavenly provision was unlike anything God's people had ever seen. Moses was probably just as amazed and curious as everyone else, but he knew one thing; this bread was from the Lord and it was supplied for the Israelites to eat. However, before anyone could begin gathering the mysterious flakes, Moses needed to relay God's instructions for handling His miraculous provision.

Read Exodus 16:16–19 and note those instructions:

An omer is probably about 2 quarts.[20] The families measured and gathered the flakes so each person had enough to sustain him for the day. The flakes weren't to be hoarded or saved. But God had more guidelines. Let's look more closely at His instructions. Read Exodus 16:20–36 and answer the questions below.

When were the Israelites to gather the manna (v. 21)? __________

What happened when the sun grew hot (v. 21)? __________

What was significant about the sixth day (v. 22)? __________

What was significant about the seventh day (v. 25)? __________

Why did God tell His people to save one omer of manna for future generations (v. 32)?

God provided exactly what the Israelites needed during their desert journey, but His people had to gather when the gathering was good. They couldn't work hard one day and then rest in the camp, eating what remained for the rest of the week. For six days, God instructed his people to gather and cook and enjoy the bread. On the sixth day, they worked twice as hard, gathering and baking and boiling. But on the seventh day, they were to rest, eat their allotted manna, and relax in the camp.

> God provided exactly what the Israelites needed during their desert journey, but His people had to gather when the gathering was good.

According to Exodus 16:35, how long did the Israelites eat manna?

As the Israelites gathered and cooked and ate their daily provision, they could never have anticipated the thin, honey-flavored wafers would be their mainstay for the next forty years. That knowledge was best left unrevealed, as the Israelites packed up and left the Desert of Sin.

Read Exodus 17:1–7.

What was the problem with the Israelites' camp at Rephidim?

What insight into Moses' feelings do you get from verse 4?

I must admit, I chuckled when I recently read this verse. Moses was exasperated. God had given him these people to lead, and despite the fact the Israelites had witnessed God's glory over and over again, the people still had the audacity to ask, "Is the Lord among us or not?" To make matters even more frustrating, they still blamed Moses for their situation. These people God had given Moses to shepherd appeared to be about as sharp as those sheep he'd herded back in Midian.

What did the Lord tell Moses to do in verse 5?

What a great response. Maybe Moses' sense of unworthiness was still holding him back as a leader. Perhaps he tried to walk in the middle of the crowd because he wasn't confident enough to walk out in front and lead the way. God basically said, "Moses, you were a shepherd. When you want to lead sheep, what do you do?" God told Moses to apply what he'd learned during his shepherding days. "Walk on ahead of the people."

Read Jesus' teachings recorded in John 10:2–4, and note what you learn about the position of a shepherd as he leads his flock.

Ladies, when God places you in a leadership role, regardless how unworthy you may feel; no matter how much you want to be just another member of the crowd, God's words to Moses can be applied to you too. "Walk on ahead of the people." You can't lead from the middle of the pack. If you don't walk ahead and lead, quarreling, grumbling, and a sense of disorder will develop among your people.

Moses knew how to lead. He'd been shepherding for forty years. It was time for Moses to be a shepherd leader for God's people, and right now, these sheep needed some water.

Look back at Exodus 17:6. What did God say would happen when Moses obeyed Him and walked ahead of the people, striking the rock at Horeb?

Look back at Exodus 12:37. How many people were in need of water?

This was a large group of people. The rock Moses struck wasn't an oversized landscaping stone. This was probably a massive rock that stood stories high on the side of Mount Horeb. Life-sustaining refreshment didn't just trickle out of the rock like water from a backyard faucet. It would take a stream of water flowing in the middle of the desert to meet the needs of a crowd this size.

Read Psalm 78:20a below:

When he struck the rock, water gushed out, and streams flowed abundantly. (NIV '84)

How did the psalmist describe the water that flowed from the rock at Mount Horeb?

Moses struck the rock and enough water came gushing forth to meet the needs of everyone in that thirsty crowd. I imagine that as those streams of God's abundant provision suddenly began flowing from that rock, applause immediately erupted from the astonished crowd.

When you face seemingly impossible circumstances and there appears to be no provision in sight, remember the rock at Horeb. For nothing is impossible with God (Luke 1:37). Our Lord owns the earth and all that is in it, and He is able to provide more than enough of what you need—even when there appears to be no answer in sight.

When you face seemingly impossible circumstances and there appears to be no provision in sight, remember the rock at Horeb.

I hope the Israelites filled their sheepskin canteens. As we will see in tomorrow's lesson, trouble was brewing on the desert horizon.

WEEK FIVE DAY TWO

Family Interventions

Moses' father-in-law replied, "What you are doing is not good."

EXODUS 18:17

Yesterday, we saw God miraculously provide for the Israelites as they traveled through the desert and eventually arrived at Mount Sinai, also called Mount Horeb. They ate manna for the first time, enjoyed quail to their hearts' content, and watched as streams of life-sustaining water flowed from a rock. But before they were able to get comfortable in their new camp, their enemy was plotting their demise.

Begin today by reading Exodus 17:8–16.

As the Amalekites descended upon the camp, Moses turned to a younger man named Joshua, a man who would become a student and companion of Moses' throughout the rest of our journey. Joshua rallied some troops, and the next morning the army forged into battle as Moses climbed to the top of a hill with the staff of God in his hands.

As the Amalekites descended upon the camp, Moses turned to a younger man named Joshua.

What name did Moses give the altar he built after this battle (v. 15)?

The Hebrew word for "banner" reflects the root "to be high," "raised," or "conspicuous."[21] Moses raised the Staff of God high, making sure every soldier recognized God's active presence in their battle. Hour by hour, Moses stood strong. When his arms grew weary and he lowered the staff, the Amalekites gained momentum. When he once again raised the staff, the Israelites regained their edge. Moses, exhausted from standing and raising that staff, finally made a chair out of a nearby stone.

According to verse 12, who came alongside Moses to help him keep the staff raised as the battle raged on into the late hours of the day?

"Jewish tradition has it that Hur was the husband of Miriam."[22] Isn't it touching to know Moses' family supported him in his service to God? The three men remained steadfast until the Israelites finally defeated their enemy. Moses held his staff heavenward, acknowledging God as the source of victory in battle. The humble leader ended his day by building an altar and naming it "The Lord is my Banner." What a touching thought. In essence, Moses said, "When people see this altar, they will know I and my people serve and honor Yahweh." Like an Olympic competitor proudly carrying his country's flag during opening ceremonies, Moses and the Israelites would honor and serve Yahweh on their journey.

Look back at Exodus 17:14. What was Moses instructed to do after the Israelites won their fight against the Amalekites?

God told Moses to make sure Joshua heard about all that happened to bring the Israelites victory in battle. Moses' new sidekick would lead many military campaigns in the years ahead and he needed to learn to rely upon God's power, not his own intellect or strength. Interestingly, Joshua wasn't the only one who heard about God's work on behalf of His people.

Moses' new sidekick would lead many military campaigns in the years ahead and he needed to learn to rely upon God's power, not his own intellect or strength.

Read Exodus 18:1–4. According to verse 1, who else heard about the things God had done?

At some point in his journey, Moses had sent Zipporah and their two boys back to Midian. Perhaps he had been concerned about their well being back in Egypt as his negotiations with Pharaoh grew increasingly hostile. I imagine Jethro and Zipporah quizzed every traveler passing through Midian as to the whereabouts of Moses because evidently Jethro and Zipporah had heard about all the Lord had done for His people.

Now, read Exodus 18:5–6. At what mountain did the Israelites set up camp?

The sight of Mount Horeb (also called Sinai) must have brought tears to our humble leader's eyes. Look back at Exodus 3:11–12. How would Moses confirm it was God who sent him to free the Israelites from bondage in Egypt?

Moses was back where it all began. I wonder if he memorized the location of the burning bush. Was there still evidence of his divine encounter? Scripture is silent about these details, but we do know Jethro and Zipporah heard Moses was back in his old shepherding territory, and they took the opportunity to join him.

Read Exodus 18:7–12.

What details of his journey did Moses share with his father-in-law (v. 8)?

After a warm family reunion, Moses and Jethro went into the tent for what I imagine was an encouraging, fatherly chat. Since the day our former-shepherd packed up and headed for Egypt, Moses probably hadn't had the opportunity to share his deepest thoughts and concerns with this man who had been an integral part of his life for forty years. Moses shared the victories of his rescue mission, but he also told Jethro about the hardships he and God's people had experienced during their desert travels. I would guess Moses expressed a vast array of emotions as he shared all he had witnessed along his journey.

According to verse 11, how did Jethro respond to Moses' testimony?

Isn't that amazing? Jethro was a priest of Midian—a nation known for its worship of idols such as Baal, who was thought to be the god of the land, owning and controlling it.[23] Yet, as Jethro listened to Moses' story, he was fully convinced the idols he had worshipped were nothing compared to the God Moses served.

When you talk to people about your faith, are you uncomfortable sharing the hardships you've endured as a follower of Christ?

Moses told Jethro about the disappointments as well as the victories he experienced as he served the Lord. When you talk to people about your faith, are you uncomfortable sharing the hardships you've endured as a follower of Christ? It's exciting to share triumphs and stories of God's incredible provision. Yet, I would guess, the reality of God's active presence in your life has probably also been evident during times of great trial or pain. A balanced, honest testimony is sometimes the most effective way to share our faith with non-Christians. Share your thoughts below:

Aaron and the elders of Israel joined Moses and Jethro for a time of worship and fellowship. It had been an emotional day, and I would guess Moses probably slept well that night, surrounded by his family. The next day, however, it was business as usual for Israel's leader, and it appears he declared it "Take your Father-in-Law to Work Day." Let's see what happened as Jethro observed Moses in action.

Read Exodus 18:13–27.

What did Jethro observe that troubled him?

According to verse 14, how long did Moses spend judging cases?

In the ancient Near East, the job of judging civil and criminal disputes went along with a leadership position.[24] Moses was Israel's representative before God. I don't think he was being prideful as he sat to judge disputes. I think his heart was right. It was Moses' method that needed some adjusting. The overworked leader made the same mistake many sincere, well intentioned servants make: He failed to train up and empower other leaders. As a result, Moses was wearing himself out and people's needs were not being met.

Moses was Israel's representative before God. I don't think he was being prideful as he sat to judge disputes. It was Moses' method that needed some adjusting.

According to verse 24, how did Moses respond to Jethro's advice?

Let's see how our budding leader implemented the plan. Read Deuteronomy 1:9–18.

Moses involved God's people in the process. He had them suggest wise, understanding and respectable men to serve as their judges (v. 13). Moses then taught his leadership and instructed them on how to carry out their duties. Most of all, he reminded them to fear God, not men, and to trust God to help them make the right rulings (v. 17).

Our heavenly Father was faithful to provide family members to support Moses as he did his best to lead God's people. God sent Jethro to correct and redirect our well-meaning leader's governing activities and Moses was growing into a humble, teachable, leader of God's people. It appears that his family recognized and supported his call to leadership, intervening as needed along the way.

WEEK FIVE DAY THREE

A Promise Fulfilled

The LORD your God has increased your numbers so that today you are as many as the stars in the sky."

DEUTERONOMY 1:9-10

Yesterday, we read about the heavy burden Moses carried as the prophet and judge for the massive group of desert wanderers, called the Israelites. God sent Jethro to help Moses recognize the need to delegate some of his responsibilities to trustworthy, god-fearing men who could help him govern the people.

To begin today's discussion, let's look again at Moses' words from Deuteronomy 1 (below) as he began the process of implementing his father-in-law's advice by appointing new leaders:

At that time I said to you, "You are too heavy a burden for me to carry alone. The LORD your God has increased your numbers so that today you are as many as the stars in the sky. Choose some wise, understanding and respected men from each of your tribes, and I will set them over you." (vv. 9-10, 13)

Now look back at God's promise to Abraham as recorded in Genesis 15:4–7.

According to verse 5, what visual did God use to communicate the vast number of offspring that would eventually descend from Abraham?

As Moses stood before the people, they must have indeed looked as numerous as the stars in the sky. God had made a covenant with Abraham hundreds of years earlier, guaranteeing His promise. The massive group of the Patriarch's descendants who were camped near Mount Sinai served as evidence that God had indeed kept His word.

With God's faithfulness fresh on his mind, Moses set up the new leadership and established a judicial system. He sent his father-in-law, Jethro, back to Midian and then Moses set his heart on a fresh encounter with His Lord. Let's see what happened as the man of God made his way up onto the mountain of God.

Read Exodus 19:3–8.

Not only had God been faithful to Abraham, He had been faithful to keep His promise to Moses as well. About a year earlier, the Lord told the insecure shepherd he and the newly freed Israelites would return to that mountain and worship Him. As Moses made his way up the rocky mountainside, he had come full circle. It was an amazing moment for the humble man who had struggled to accept His calling. Moses approached the top of the mountain and Yahweh, Moses' promise-keeping Lord, had a message for the house of Jacob (referring to their heritage) and the people of Israel (a reminder of the nation they had become).

According to verse 4, what did God want the Israelites to remember?

God's people had seen Him move on their behalf in Egypt, provide for them throughout their journey, and empower them in a battle against their enemy. In essence, God had carried them "on eagles' wings"—not just to a safe desert location at the foot of a mountain, but into His very presence at the mountain of God.

God is immutable. He never changes, and there is nothing in His nature that can change. He is the same today as He was when He first made his covenant with Abraham and when He parted the Red Sea for Moses. The same God who provided manna for His people to eat in the desert is the same God who chooses to manifest His active presence in the circumstances of ***your*** life today.

God is immutable. He never changes, and there is nothing in His nature that can change.

How has God manifested His active presence in your circumstances? Maybe He has provided groceries for your family when your bank account was empty and your pantry shelves were bare. Perhaps He comforted you through a difficult loss. Has He led you to a church where you can grow and serve Him? Has He provided a compassionate, loving teacher to show the love of Jesus to your less-than-focused child? Fill in the blank below with brief description of one instance when you were aware of God's glorious work in your life. Then personalize His words to the Israelites:

You yourself have seen what I did

____

and how I carried you on eagles' wings and brought you to myself.

The Israelites could depend on God, and you can depend on Him today as well. Your Lord is constant, immutable, and reliable. As a believer in Christ, you can have a Mount Sinai moment with God at any time. You don't have to trek up a mountain to be in His presence. You can sit in a comfortable chair early in the morning before anyone in your house stirs. You can pour out your heart to your Lord as you run a marathon or walk in your neighborhood. As a matter of fact, you can have a Mount Sinai moment with your Lord right now. You personally experience His glory when you recognize His activity in the everyday circumstances of your life.

> The Israelites could depend on God, and you can depend on Him today as well.

Pause for a moment to worship your Lord by writing a prayer of thanksgiving on the lines below.

____

____

Moses worshipped His Lord and then made the trek back down to the mountain to deliver the good news. God was inviting His people to make a covenant with Him. If they kept it, they would be a kingdom of priests and a holy nation, set apart and treasured by God.

According to Exodus 19:8, how did the people respond?

____

The Israelites were thrilled. God wanted them to be priests; His representatives to the world around them. The people readily agreed, and Moses (probably a little tired from all the climbing) made his way back up Mount Sinai, once again, to relay the people's enthusiasm.

Read Exodus 19:9–17.

Moses descended the mountain one last time that day to deliver ***Yahweh's*** message and prepare the people to enter His presence three days later at the foot of Mount Sinai. What did God tell Moses to do prior to this all-important meeting at the mountain (v. 10)?

The Hebrew word translated "consecrate" in this verse is ***qadhesh*** and it means "to be set apart" (i.e., from that which is common or unclean). God wanted His people set apart and undistracted by everything common around them. They were instructed to wash their clothes and abstain from sexual intimacy with a husband or wife. The central focus for the entire nation was the invitation to stand in the very presence of Yahweh at Mount Sinai.

Anticipation must have been building among the people until, finally, dawn broke on the third day. Lightening flashed, and thunder erupted as a dark cloud hovered over the mountain. Suddenly they heard it—the awaited trumpet blast summoned Moses to gather the people at the foot of the mountain.

Read Exodus 19:18–25. Try to imagine yourself among the Israelites.

Can you smell the scent of brush burning as smoke billows up from the mountain? Can you feel the ground tremble and hear the trumpet blasts growing louder and louder? Suddenly, the voice of the Lord penetrates the atmosphere. Yahweh is among you and He summons Moses to the top of the mountain.

Look back at Exodus 19:9. What was God's purpose for His awe inspiring descent upon Mount Sinai?

Now, take a peek back at Exodus 4:1. What was Moses' primary concern back when God first commissioned him to free the Israelites?

God was so faithful to Moses. As the people stood around that mountain, there was no doubt in any of their minds; God indeed appeared to Moses. As their appointed leader

> As their appointed leader stepped down off Mount Sinai into the crowd, I imagine the people listened to him a little more intently. They needed to listen.

stepped down off Mount Sinai into the crowd, I imagine the people listened to him a little more intently. They needed to listen. As we will see in tomorrow's lesson, God was about to personally deliver His commandments and laws.

WEEK FIVE | **DAY FOUR**

Mountainous Commandments

"Then God gave the people all these instructions."

Exodus 20:1 NLT

When we closed yesterday's lesson, the Israelites were gathered around Mount Sinai. They had agreed to enter into a covenant with God and were awaiting His instructions. Moses had just finished speaking with the Lord and returned to the base of the mountain, warning people not to break through the barriers he had set up around Mount Sinai.

According to Exodus 3:5, what were God's instructions the last time Moses had been at this site?

____

____

> Yahweh had descended upon the mountain and Horeb was once again holy ground.

Moses delivered a similar message. The people of Israel were not to go any closer. Yahweh had descended upon the mountain and Horeb was once again holy ground. We don't know if the people removed their sandals, but after Moses finished speaking, the cleaned up crowd of former slaves heard the voice of God for themselves as He outlined the terms of His covenant. The mandates God relayed directly to His people that day from the top of Mount Sinai are called the Ten Commandments.

Please read Exodus 20:1–17 and summarize each of the Ten Commandments in your own words. I've listed the first two for you.

1. Worship only Yahweh.

2. Do not create any type of idol for yourselves.

3. __________

4. __________

5. __________

6. __________

7. __________

8. __________

9. __________

10. __________

Other than the command to rest on the Sabbath, God's commandments addressed the Israelites' relationship with Him as well as their relationships with the people around them. Look back at your list of the Ten Commandments and categorize them into vertical commandments (those governing their interaction with God) and horizontal commandments (the mandates for interacting with others). Place a "V" next to commandments involving the Israelites' interaction with God or an "H" next to the laws for interacting with people.

In your opinion, why do you think God might have chosen to set up more horizontal commands than vertical ones?

____

____

The terms of God's covenant weren't delivered through the prophet Moses. Each Israelite heard God speak with his own ears. Each person saw the lightning, heard the blaring trumpet, felt the earth tremble, and smelled the smoke that engulfed the mountain. The Israelites not only saw the glory of God that day; they experienced it. They stood in the presence of their Lord as He "spoke all these words" (Exodus 20:1) and outlined His expectations for them.

Please read Exodus 20:18–21 and note how the people reacted to their encounter with God:

___

___

The Israelites watched as Moses once again climbed Mount Sinai and disappeared into the thick dark cloud where God's presence hovered over the top of the mountain. Let's see what else God had to say through his servant, Moses.

Please read Exodus 20:22—21:1.

The Lord went on to outline additional laws governing the treatment of servants, the handling of disputes, and social interactions among God's people. He also expanded upon the foundational Ten Commandments and then assured Moses His angel would prepare the way before His people as they battled the nations to take possession of their promised land.

Now read Exodus 24:3–8.

I imagine Moses came back down the mountain that evening filled with enthusiasm about the covenant God was establishing with the Israelites. The next morning, he built an altar, supervised sacrifices, and wrote God's laws down in what the passionate leader called, The Book of the Covenant.

> I imagine Moses came back down the mountain that evening filled with enthusiasm about the covenant God was establishing with the Israelites.

With the terms of the covenant defined, the people agreed to "do everything" the Lord said. Moses sprinkled blood on the altar (representing God) as well as on the people. The covenant was confirmed. This agreement required the Israelites' adherence to the terms of the covenant. Look back at Exodus 19:5–6 and note the blessing God offered to the Israelites if they did, indeed, keep His covenant:

___

___

Israel was to be set apart as God's people, a kingdom of priests who would represent Him to the world around them. They were to be God's treasured possession. The people thought they could keep the terms of the covenant; however, God knew they couldn't.

Israel was to be set apart as God's people, a kingdom of priests who would represent Him to the world around them.

What does Romans 3:20 tell you about the law?

Look back at Exodus 20:20. What was the reason God spoke directly to the people from Mount Sinai?

The law was established to make people aware of God's expectations and their inability to meet those expectations. That knowledge would lay the foundation for God's ultimate plan of salvation through His Son, Jesus.

As a way of closing today's lesson, read Deuteronomy 4:5–12 and note what other nations would deduct about God from the behavior and lifestyle of His people:

The way God's people choose to live makes an impression (good or bad) on the people with whom we come in contact. Just as the Israelites left an altar behind at Mount Sinai declaring the Lord as their banner, we in essence carry a banner with the Lord's name on it whenever we make people aware of our faith. May our behavior, more often than not, reflect the wisdom and gracious nature of our Lord.

The Israelite families probably made their way back to their individual tents that evening with their hearts set on being called a holy nation and a treasured possession. I imagine the blood stains on their clothing were poignant reminders of the words they heard thundering from atop Mount Sinai. The nation wanted to be faithful. Sadly, God knew they wouldn't be. For the people of Israel and even for us today, those laws were mountainous commandments laid forth by a holy, yet abundantly merciful God.

The way God's people choose to live makes an impression (good or bad) on the people with whom we come in contact.

WEEK FIVE DAY FIVE

Personal Application

Application for Days One and Two

After God provided abundantly and brought the Israelites victory in their battle against the Amalekites, Moses built an altar and named it, "The Lord is My Banner." That altar stood as a memorial acknowledging Yahweh as Israel's God and protector before every other nation that would later pass by Mount Sinai.

Interestingly, a similar thought process led to the decision to mark United States currency with the words, "In God We Trust." It all began with a man who, like Moses, wanted the world to know God was his nation's divine protector. The following is an excerpt from a letter written in 1861 to Secretary of the Treasury, Salmon P. Chase, by Reverend M.R. Watkinson:

> "You are probably a Christian. What if our Republic were not shattered beyond reconstruction? Would not the antiquaries of succeeding centuries rightly reason from our past that we were a heathen nation?"

Reverend Watkinson then proposed a coin design that included the words, GOD, LIBERTY, LAW. He said:

> "This would relieve us from the ignominy of heathenism. This would place us openly under the Divine protection we have personally claimed."

As a result of Reverend Watkinson's letter, Secretary Chase asked the Director of the mint at Philadelphia to prepare a motto and stated the following in a letter dated November 20, 1861:

> "Dear Sir: No nation can be strong except in the strength of God, or safe except in His defense. The trust of our people in God should be declared on our national coins."

Several mottos were considered, and then finally, in December of 1863, Secretary Chase, suggested the motto, IN GOD WE TRUST. The Congress passed the Act of April 22, 1864, and IN GOD WE TRUST first appeared on the 1864 two-cent coin. [25]

Take Moses' example and the words of Reverend Watkinson personally for a moment. If your neighborhood were destroyed by a national disaster and the site where your home stands was excavated hundreds of years from now, what evidence would exist of your family's faith? I'd like to challenge you to take a few moments to come up with a short motto you and your family might adopt as a witness to others and a reminder to one another of your dependence upon and trust in God. Have fun with this and write your motto on the lines that follow:

I'd like to challenge you to take a few moments to come up with a short motto you and your family might adopt as a witness to others and a reminder to one another of your dependence upon and trust in God.

____

____

____

____

If you are doing this study with others, share your motto or brainstorm options with members of your group.

Application for Days Three and Four

In Day Three, as Moses began the process of selecting his new leadership, he looked around at the massive crowd and realized God had been faithful to make Abraham's descendants as numerous as the stars in the sky. Yahweh fulfilled that promise and, therefore, His people could count on Him to bring His other promises to pass as well. If you recall, God took the sole responsibility for keeping His covenant with Abraham.

Read Hebrews 6:13–17.

According to verse 17, what was the reason God confirmed His promise with an oath?

____

____

As the Israelites looked around at the masses of people, they could see that God had kept His promise to make Abraham's descendants as numerous as the stars in the sky. The Lord entered into that one-sided covenant with Abraham so His people would recognize the unchanging nature of His purpose.

To get a better idea of God's unchanging purpose for His people, let's look back at God's original promise to Abraham when He commissioned the Patriarch and brought him out of Ur of the Chaldeans. Read Genesis 12:1–3 below.

"I will make you into a great nation and I will bless you; I will make your name great, and you will be a blessing. I will bless those who bless you, and whoever curses you I will curse; and all peoples on earth will be blessed through you." (emphasis added)

God promised to be the God of Abraham's descendants.

God promised to be the God of Abraham's descendants. He also swore to give them the land of Canaan; the promised land. The Israelites could count on the Lord to keep those promises just as surely as He was faithful to multiply them into what had become the nation of Israel.

As Yahweh made His covenant with Abraham, the promise was for Abraham and his offspring (Genesis 12:7, 13:15). In the original language, the word translated here as offspring is the Hebrew word "***zera.***" It means seed. Figuratively, it means fruit, plant, sowing-time, posterity. There was one particular offspring or "Seed" the Sovereign Lord had in mind as he made His covenant with Abraham and it is through that Seed all the nations of the world would be blessed.

Let's see how the apostle Paul explains the unchanging purpose of God which led to His covenant with Abraham, but also prompted Him to establish the Mosaic covenant (represented by the Ten Commandments) with His people at Mount Sinai.

Read Galatians 3:15–25 from your Bible and then, for clarification, read Galatians 3:19 from the New Living Translation below:

Why, then, was the law given? It was given alongside the promise to show people their sins. But the law was designed to last only until the coming of the child who was promised.

As Moses sprinkled the people of Israel with the blood of covenant, Yahweh—the active and present covenant keeper—knew the people couldn't keep His law. He had a plan in place. The Seed (Jesus) would one day come, cover the sins of the world with the shedding of His blood, and free them from the penalty and imprisonment of the Mosaic Law. The law was temporary; given to reveal sin and make all of us aware of our inability to meet God's expectations so we would recognize our need for a Savior.

Review your list of the Ten Commandments on page 103. Now read Romans 8:1–2 and note what assurance you have through Christ:

____

____

Before Christ, we were held prisoners by the law (Galatians 3:23); however, through faith in Jesus Christ, we are freed from the law of sin and death. Regardless of our inability to meet God's standards, we are not condemned.

Before Christ, we were held prisoners by the law (Galatians 3:23); however, through faith in Jesus Christ, we are freed from the law of sin and death.

Have you accepted Jesus as your Lord and Savior? If not, will you consider doing so today? All you have to do is accept the free gift of salvation our Jesus offers you.

Read Romans 10:9, and then pray this prayer with me now:

> Yahweh, Father, I believe that Jesus is your Son, who came to this earth as a man and died on a cross for my sins. I acknowledge to you that I am a sinner and I need forgiveness. Your Word says in Romans 10:9, "That if [I] confess with [my] mouth, 'Jesus is Lord,' and believe in [my] heart that God raised him from the dead, [I] will be saved." I do believe, Lord, and I take Jesus today as my personal Lord and Savior. Thank you, Father, for saving me from the law of sin and death. In Jesus' name I pray.

If you prayed that prayer for the first time, please talk to your small group leader or pastor. Rejoice in the fact you are not condemned. You are free, cleansed in the blood of Christ.

Interestingly, once our sins were cleansed by the blood of Christ, God is faithful to keep another promise He made to His people at Mount Sinai.

How are believers in Christ described in 1 Peter 2:9:

____

____

As a way of closing, take a few moments to praise God for the privilege of being His treasured possession as part of His priesthood of believers.

Week 6

The Tent of Meeting

WEEK SIX DAY ONE

Reverent Responses

God's Message: "Heaven's my throne, earth is my footstool . . .
I made all this! I own all this!"
God's Decree. "But there is something I'm looking for: a person simple and plain, reverently responsive to what I say.

ISAIAH 66:1–2 MSG

In last week's lesson, we observed the people of Israel having a divine encounter with Yahweh when He descended upon Mount Sinai. The crowd heard God thunder down the Ten Commandments from atop the mountain. They felt the earth quake, saw the consuming fire, and smelled the lingering smoke. The people remained at a distance; feared for their lives and asked their blossoming leader to speak as God's representative in the future. Moses then went back up onto the mountain. When he returned, he read the people what he called, the Book of the Covenant, which contained more of God's laws and expectations. Moses then reminded

God's people of the importance of keeping the covenant and sprinkled the crowd with blood, confirming the nation's agreement to live in accordance with God's laws.

Let's see how their day ended. Please read Exodus 24:9–11.

Moses, Aaron, and his two oldest sons (Exodus 6:23), along with seventy Israelite elders climbed back up onto Mount Sinai. According to verse 10, what did these leaders see?

____

____

Read the verses below and note any additional information you learn about what these men might have seen as they stood with Moses on Mount Sinai.

Exodus 33:19–20: ____

Ezekiel 1:25–28: ____

____

Revelation 4: 1–3, 6: ____

____

No one has ever actually seen God in all His glory, but our Lord allowed these leaders to see a hint of His magnificent presence as they ate a meal together, which was customary when establishing a covenant.

Now read the Lord's words from Isaiah 66:1–2 at the beginning of today's lesson. My friend, our Lord is always on His throne. And whether you describe it as a pavement of sapphire or a sea of glass, His holy feet somehow rest upon an expanse similar to what we call the sky. He is in control. His presence is so almighty and awesome we humans can't possibly see Him in all His fullness and live. But He watches for someone like our Moses had become; a simple, plain and ordinary person who reverently responded to His voice. Will that be you? Will you listen and respond to His voice? Will you do your best to obey His commands and honor Him as holy and righteous and merciful? When you do, like these leaders who were amazed they weren't struck dead by a

Our Lord is always on His throne. And whether you describe it as a pavement of sapphire or a sea of glass, His holy feet somehow rest upon an expanse similar to what we call the sky. He is in control.

mere glance at a shadow of His presence, God will allow you to witness His glory in our world. He will make you more aware of His power and His character. He will invite you to commune with Him.

Look at God's next words to Moses in Exodus 24:12. What did God invite Moses to do?

God said, "Come up to me on the mountain and stay here . . ." He invited His simple, plain, reverently responsive man of God to come and stay with Him for a while on the mountain of God. Before we move forward with the rest of our lesson, let's practice staying in God's presence. First, note the current time: ______________________. Now take five minutes (just five minutes) without reading, or writing anything and simply commune with your Lord. Because of the blood shed for you by God the Son, you are invited to stay in the presence of God the Father. No words are adequate. Just rest in His holy presence.

If you are still awake (Naps in His presence are sometimes God-ordained as well), note your thoughts regarding your five-minute stay in God's presence:

What a poignant ending to an eventful day at the now infamous Mount Sinai. Israel's reverently responsive shepherd leader wasted no time in taking God up on His offer. Let's see what happened as Moses climbed the mountain of God once again.

Read Exodus 24:12–18.

Moses told his brother Aaron, his brother-in-law Hur, and the elders to wait there at the base of Mount Sinai until he returned. According to verse 14, what duty did Moses assign to Aaron and Hur in his absence?

Aaron and Hur were commissioned with leadership duties and then Moses and his newly appointed aide, Joshua, climbed up onto the mountain at the Lord's request.

> God presented His passionate servant leader with the blueprints for a special tent that would be a portable sanctuary—a place where God's people could worship Him.

After a six day stay, Moses had a divine meeting with Yahweh on the mountain. The Lord not only gave him the stone tablets with the Ten Commandments, as He promised, but He continued to teach Moses about worship. This meeting had a special purpose. God presented His passionate servant leader with the blueprints for a special tent that would be a portable sanctuary—a place where God's people could worship Him. The glory of the Lord would dwell in this tent, just as His people lived in portable tents while traveling through the wilderness toward their Promised Land.

Let's see what God had planned for this distinctive structure. Read Exodus 25:1–9.

What items were to be given at this special offering for God's sanctuary?

According to verse 2, who was to give offerings for the construction of the tabernacle?

Everyone whose heart prompted him to give was to supply the materials for the construction of God's sanctuary. Interestingly, God Himself had provided all of these materials for His people along their journey. The gold, silver, and bronze had been given to the Hebrews as they exited Egypt. "Egypt excelled in the production of twined linen, where every thread was twisted from many strands."[26] I would guess the Hebrews learned the Egyptian art over the years. The yarn and fine linen probably also resulted from the Israelite's time in slavery. The goat hair, ram skins, sea cow hides, and acacia wood were probably gathered along their journey through the Red Sea and the Sinai Peninsula. Perhaps the oil, spices, and onyx stones were plundered from the Amalekites or accumulated through trading. Somehow, God had supplied His people with all of the materials necessary to build a place where His glory would dwell among them. But each person had to respond to the Lord's invitation to give.

Somehow, God had supplied His people with all of the materials necessary to build a place where His glory would dwell among them. But each person had to respond to the Lord's invitation to give.

Look back at Isaiah 66:1–2 again (Beginning of Lesson). What did God say about the things of this world?

The first act of worship associated with the tabernacle would be an offering for the construction. God made it clear, no one was obligated. This was a freewill offering. The earth is His. He owns it all. Our Lord could have demanded they give, but He wanted every thread of fabric and article of gold to represent His treasured people's reverent response of heartfelt worship.

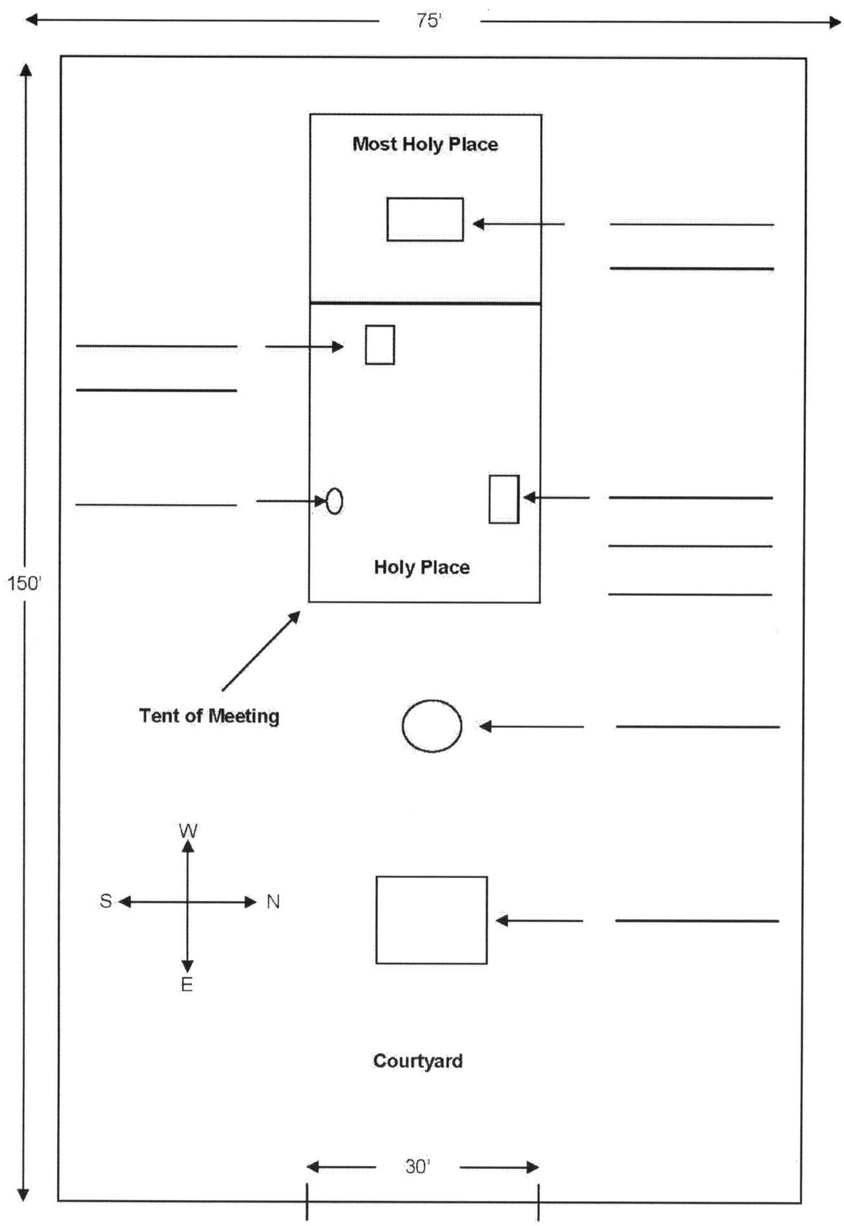

The Plan of the Tabernacle

Read 2 Corinthians 9:7. What attitude does God desire when bringing an offering to Him?

A little later in our story, Moses invites the people to give for the sanctuary, just as God commanded. Let's peek ahead for a moment and see how they responded. Read Exodus 35:20–29.

What a beautiful outpouring of worship. Men and women alike brought jewelry of all kinds. Those with the requested linens and animal skins willingly brought them. The skilled women spun yarn or fine linens. The simple, plain desert travelers, who had spent years in captivity, reverently and graciously responded to what the Lord requested through Moses. Worship is our theme this week. Tomorrow, we'll take look at the layout of the sanctuary as revealed to Moses during his forty day stay in the Lord's glorious presence on Mount Sinai.

WEEK SIX DAY TWO

The Holiest of Grounds

You shall consecrate them so they will be most holy,
and whatever touches them will be holy.

EXODUS 30:29

When we last saw Moses, he was entering the thick cloud at the top of Mount Sinai as He went up to meet with God. As we discussed in Day One, it was during this forty-day meeting that God presented Moses with the Ten Commandments, written on the famous tablets of stone. However, there was another purpose for the meeting. God revealed the blueprints for an amazing structure called the Tabernacle; a special tent where

God's glory would dwell with His people as they traveled through the wilderness en route to their promised land. The detailed guidelines for the Tabernacle's construction span from Exodus 25:10 through 40:33. Don't panic! I won't have you read all of those chapters today. Instead, we are going to read select passages and identify the components of the Tabernacle as pictured in the diagram on page 115. Take a moment to look at the diagram before continuing with our lesson.

Moses was commissioned with the task of overseeing the Tabernacle's construction. In a moment, we'll read God's directives to His humble general contractor and identify each element of the portable sanctuary. Please read the passages, underline the materials used, and try to visualize the structure by referencing the Tabernacle diagram.

Moses was commissioned with the task of overseeing the Tabernacle's construction.

The Courtyard:

The Curtain: ***For the entrance to the courtyard, provide a curtain twenty cubits long, of blue, purple and scarlet yarn and finely twisted linen—the work of an embroiderer—with four posts and four bases.*** (Exodus 27:16)

The Structure: ***All the posts around the courtyard are to have silver bands and hooks, and bronze bases. The courtyard shall be a hundred cubits long and fifty cubits wide, with curtains of finely twisted linen five cubits[c] high, and with bronze bases.*** (Exodus 27:17–18)

Tent of Meeting:

Exterior Curtains: ***Make the tabernacle with ten curtains of finely twisted linen and blue, purple and scarlet yarn, with cherubim worked into them by a skilled craftsman. All the curtains are to be the same size—twenty-eight cubits long and four cubits wide.*** (Exodus 26:1–2)

Tent Covering: ***Make for the tent a covering of ram skins dyed red, and over that a covering of hides of sea cows.*** (Exodus 26:14)

Inner Curtain: ***Make a curtain of blue, purple and scarlet yarn and finely twisted linen, with cherubim worked into it by a skilled craftsman. Hang it with gold hooks on four posts of acacia wood overlaid with gold and standing on four silver bases. Hang the curtain from the clasps and place the ark of the Testimony behind the curtain. The curtain will separate the Holy Place from the Most Holy Place.*** (Exodus 26:31–33)

What chambers did this curtain separate?

WEEK SIX

All of these curtains, frames, and bases created the basic structure for the Tabernacle. Now let's identify the contents of the courtyard and then the Tent of Meeting. We will record them in the order they appear from the entrance to the courtyard into the Most Holy Place. Read the passages below, answer the questions, and locate each holy furnishing on your diagram.

The Altar of Burnt Offering: Read Exodus 27:1–5.

Of what was the altar constructed?

This was an altar for animal sacrifices and the place where animal meat was cooked.[27]

The Basin: Read Exodus 30:17–21.

Of what was the basin constructed, and what was its purpose?

The Table for the Bread of the Presence: Read Exodus 25:23–30.

Of what was the table constructed?

What was placed on this special table and how often was it to be there?

Read Leviticus 24:5–6 and note how this bread was arranged:

The bread was to remain in the presence of God at all times. Even when the Tabernacle was transported during the Israelites' travels, the bread was covered and remained in the same arrangement.

The Lampstand: Read Exodus 25:31–40.

Of what was the lampstand constructed (v. 31) and what was its purpose (v. 37)?

Exodus 27:20–21: Who was to keep the lamps burning and during what time frame?

The Altar of Incense: Read Exodus 30:1–3, 6.

Of what was the altar constructed and where was it placed?

Exodus 30:7–8: When was incense to be burned on the altar?

The Ark of the Covenant (or Testimony):

Exodus 25:10–11, 17–22: Of what was the ark constructed?

Read verse 21 below and circle the item that was to be placed inside the ark:

You shall put the mercy seat on the top of the ark, and in the ark you shall put the Testimony [the Ten Commandments] that I will give you. (Exodus 25:21 AMP)

Read verse 22 again. What do you think Moses would have considered most significant about the Ark of the Testimony?

Everything inside the sanctuary structure had to be pure and clean. The entire Tabernacle was considered holy and was only to be used for God's distinct purposes. To emphasize this point, once the plans were conveyed for all of the tent's contents, the Lord instructed Moses to set apart and consecrate everything in His sacred sanctuary.

The entire Tabernacle was considered holy and was only to be used for God's distinct purposes.

Read Exodus 30:22–29.

Consecration is an act by which a person or thing is dedicated to the service and worship of God. The Hebrew word ***qadhesh***, translated consecrate, means to be set apart (i.e. from that which is common or unclean).[28] God instructed Moses to set apart this structure and the priests who would serve there for His purposes.

According to verse 29, what would happen to whatever touched the consecrated components of God's sacred sanctuary?

Once the construction project was complete, Moses was to anoint everything inside the courtyard walls. Considering the definition of consecration, why do you think the outer perimeter of the Tabernacle's courtyard was not anointed?

Everything inside the finely twisted linens of the courtyard walls would be holy, set apart for God's purposes. Moses was even instructed to anoint Aaron and his sons, who would serve as priests in the sacred sanctuary.

The Hebrew word translated "tabernacle" in the passages we read today means, "residence, dwelling place, habitation, tabernacle, tent" (Strongs). The Lord commissioned Moses to build a tabernacle, a place where God's glory could dwell among His people. Heaven is God's throne and the earth is His footstool. He created it all and owns it all (Isaiah 66:1). He didn't need a place in which to reside, but our Lord pursues intimacy with His people. He created us in His image (Genesis 1:26). Our spirits are designed to connect with His Spirit. Our Lord wanted His people to feel connected to Him and recognize His active presence among them. The tents in which the Israelites lived were common and ordinary. The tent where their Lord dwelled was the holiest of grounds in the Israelite camp. The Lord was among them, dwelling in a holy tabernacle with His treasured people in the wilderness.

WEEK SIX | DAY THREE

Wayward Worship

When Moses approached the camp and saw the calf and the dancing, his anger burned and he threw the tablets out of his hands, breaking them to pieces at the foot of the mountain.

Exodus 32:19

Yesterday we took a peek at God's blue print for His sacred wilderness sanctuary called the Tabernacle. The Lord had provided all of the materials necessary to build the holy structure, and Moses was to act as the general contractor for the project. While their leader was soaking in all of the specifics for this beautiful, sacred tent, the Israelite people grew impatient, and their hearts went grievously astray.

Please read Exodus 32:1–6.

Who cast the idol in the shape of the golden calf?

Look closely at verse 5. After Aaron built an altar in front of the calf, to whom did he say the festival would honor?

> It's difficult for us to imagine how Aaron could have possibly created an idol in Moses' absence.

It's difficult for us to imagine how Aaron could have possibly created an idol in Moses' absence or what in the ancient world these people were thinking when they credited a calf with the dynamic works of Yahweh. I'm grieved by the thought of these people, who God loved and freed from slavery, sacrificing and honoring a golden calf as they feasted and held a festival in Yahweh's name. The Israelites' tents may have been camped in the same location at the base of Mount Sinai, but their hearts had taken a treacherous trip back to Egypt. It appears their interim leader acted as the travel agent.

After reading these passages with bewilderment, I found some information that might shed some light on this confusing and outrageous scene at the foot of the mountain. Bull cults had been popular in Egypt for thousands of years. The Apis Bull was the focus of the most popular of all the bull cults in Egypt and, unlike other idols that were thought to simply be a link to a god, the Apis was thought to actually host the god himself. In fact, when an Apis bull died, the body was embalmed and buried with full honors in a manner befitting royalty.[29] Could it be that Aaron and the Israelites were drawing from the idyllic culture of their past and somehow believed the calf was a host to the same God who had freed them from Egypt? We don't know for sure, but the explanation certainly seems plausible.

The Israelites had just heard the Ten Commandments from the mouth of God Himself. Read Exodus 20:4 below:

You shall not make for yourself an idol in the form of anything in heaven above or on earth beneath or in the waters below.

We should never underestimate the power an idol can gain in our hearts. May the scene at the base of Mount Sinai serve as a reminder to us that God's laws are not simply a list of rules to restrict His people. Living according to God's commands is what is best for us. When we let our hearts become entangled by the things of this world, those idols gain holds on us that are not easily broken. The Israelites had spent four hundred years in a culture riddled with idol worship. In the absence of a strong leader committed to the one and only true God, the newly freed Hebrews quickly sought out a familiar object for comfort and a sense of security.

We should never underestimate the power an idol can gain in our hearts.

Read Exodus 20:5. How did God describe Himself?

God isn't jealous *of* anyone or anything. He doesn't need to be. Godly jealousy means our Lord is jealous *for us* to know Him and worship Him alone. Only when our hearts are captivated by Him can we truly be liberated in Him. The Israelites had been freed from physical slavery in Egypt, but until they set their hearts on God alone, they were still prisoners to the deceptive, sinful philosophies of Egypt.

Look back at Exodus 32:6. What did the people do after presenting their offerings in front of the calf and sharing a meal?

Revelry is "any extreme intemperance and lustful indulgence, usually accompanying pagan worship."[30] This festival was not simply a misguided party. This was probably a drunken orgy at the base of the mountain God once referred to as holy ground.

Now, please read Exodus 32:7–20.

According to verses 9–10, how did the Lord respond to the Israelites' rebellious revelry?

How did Moses respond as he came down the mountain and saw the wayward partiers for himself?

Moses' big ol' heart was probably as broken as those stone tablets at the foot of the mountain. His grief manifested itself in the form of righteous indignation. The formerly insecure leader immediately took control of the unruly crowd. I imagine the music stopped and every eye became fixed on this "fellow Moses" who personally spoke to the God who brought plague after plague upon the Egyptians. The people should have been trembling with fear as Moses ground up that calf and scattered the powder into the God-provided stream that was still pouring from the rock there at Horeb. Moses was furious, but more importantly, the Lord was angry as well.

According to Exodus 32:21–24. what was Aaron's explanation?

Aaron blamed the people for his actions and came up with a ludicrous (and untrue!) explanation. The Lord was angry enough to destroy everyone involved and start over with Moses to create the nation He had promised to Abraham. However, Moses, our compassionate protagonist, felt compelled to intervene. Let's see how he handled the situation. Please read Exodus 32:25–35.

These are difficult passages to read and understand. God's people had entered into the Mosaic Covenant of the law and were subject to the condemnation their inability to meet it demanded. However, Moses stood at the entrance to the camp and gave everyone an opportunity to re-align themselves with Yahweh.

According to verse 26, who responded?

____

____

____

> Israel had become a "laughingstock" to their enemies and the majority of the people were unwilling to repent.

Sadly, only the Levites, Moses and Aaron's own tribe, responded. Israel had become a "laughingstock" to their enemies and the majority of the people were unwilling to repent. The Levites were charged with the gruesome task of killing neighbors, brothers, and even sons who were unwilling to turn back to their Lord. Moses' heart was probably heavy as he climbed back up the mountain to see if he could make atonement for the nation's sin. Israel's shepherd leader remained on the mountain, interceding for God's people, for forty days and nights (Deuteronomy 9:18–19).

Look again at Exodus 32:31–32. What did Moses offer to make atonement for the Israelites' sin?

____

In the Hebrew, the word translated ***atonement*** in verse 30 means "to cover (specifically with tar or pitch); figuratively, it means to expiate, placate or cancel" (Strongs). Moses was basically saying, "Lord, if you won't blot out their sin, then blot me out of the book you've written. Erase ***me*** in their place.

Look at Psalm 69:28. What is this book Moses was probably talking about and who is listed in it?

____

Moses offered up himself in place of his brother and the rest of the Israelites. He begged God to forgive their sin. How did God respond to Moses' offer (Exodus 32:33–34)?

Dear sisters, Moses' big-hearted offer was a foreshadowing of the atoning sacrifice of God's own Son, Jesus, on the cross. Jesus took our place—took the punishment (death) that our inability to live according to God's law demanded. He took it upon Himself. As the Passover Lamb He covered ***us*** in His blood so we could be acceptable and death would pass over us. He gave His life so we could have our names included in the Book of Life even though we all have sinned and often fall short of the glory of God (Romans 3:23).

Moses' big-hearted offer was a foreshadowing of the atoning sacrifice of God's own Son.

We, like the Israelites, succumb to wayward worship whenever we allow things or people or even our work to take the place God alone is supposed to have in our hearts. We may not understand all that happened as we study the Israelites' journey through the desert with Moses, but one thing is clear: The Lord was active and present and involved in the lives of His people. The same is true today. That truth should draw us away from the grievous sin of wayward idol worship. Our Lord is the only One worthy of our devotion.

SIX

WEEK SIX | **DAY FOUR**

Extraordinary Glory

Then Moses said, "Now show me your glory."

EXODUS 33:18

After the scenes we studied in yesterday's session, today's material will be a welcome change of pace. When the morning sun rose over Horeb the next morning, there were fewer footprints in the dry dusty sand around the base of Mount Sinai. There were also fewer complaints among the previously disgruntled travelers.

Please read Exodus 33:1–6.

Why did God say He would not go on the journey, but would instead send an angel ahead of them?

As a child, I always thought being sent to my room was an odd punishment. I had toys, books, music albums (Yes, I'm revealing my age!), and even a pet parakeet. It wasn't a terrible place to spend a few minutes. However, as a parent, I recognized the "go to your room" punishment is often a merciful act on a parent's part. Yes, the time in their rooms gave my children a chance to think about what they'd done, but it also kept me from unleashing the full brunt of my anger upon my beloved, but sometimes unruly offspring. Likewise, God mercifully withheld His wrath from His beloved children. An angel would go before them and drive out their enemies, but sadly, there would be no more pillar of cloud by day or pillar of fire by night leading the Israelites as they traveled.

What did God tell the people to take off while He decided what to do with them (vs. 5)?

Interestingly, the last time this crowd was instructed to take off their jewelry, it was used to create the idol that put them in this position in the first place. Last time, they removed their jewelry to indulge in sin. This time, they removed it to symbolize remorse for their sin.

Now read Exodus 33:7–11.

This was not the Tabernacle structure God relayed to Moses back on Mount Sinai. This was a simple tent—a representation of the sacred sanctuary. Moses would set it up "some distance away" and God's glory would descend to meet with Moses. When their leader entered his "tent of meeting" this day and the familiar pillar of cloud descended upon the entrance, the people watched from a distance, standing at the entrance to their own tents. They worshipped, and I imagine they grieved the loss of God's active presence within the camp.

Sin has consequences. As believers in Christ, God's presence is with us continually by means of His Holy Spirit, who never leaves us. However, our sin does create distance in our relationship with our Lord. What do you learn from the following passages about the way our behavior impacts the Holy Spirit within us?

1 Corinthians 6:18–20: ______________________________

____

Ephesians 4:29–31: ______________________________

____

WEEK SIX

The words we use should be beneficial and build up people around us. The Holy Spirit is grieved when we display bitterness, have fits of rage, or engage in malicious gossip. Our behavior should be upright and, as the temple of the Holy Spirit, we shouldn't do anything to dishonor God with our bodies. Sin has consequences, and we can expect to feel distance in our relationship with our Lord when we grieve His Holy Spirit.

The words we use should be beneficial and build up people around us.

Let's listen in on the conversation that took place at Moses' mock Tent of Meeting.

Read Exodus 33:12–16. What request did Moses make of God in verse 13?

____

____

Moses was a bit weary and frustrated. The Israelites were grumpy. God's glory had been withdrawn from His people. As the compassionate and conscientious leader came before God, he was overcome with emotion. Things weren't going well and Moses took full responsibility. He begged God, "teach me your ways." Moses wanted more than anything to know God more fully and lead in a way that pleased Him. The passionate leader wanted God to once again manifest His active presence among the nation the Lord called His own.

How did the Lord respond, according to verse 14?

As if he was so worked up he didn't even hear God's response, Moses kept right on talking, begging God not to send His people any further without His presence. In his emotional plea, Moses revealed the deepest longing of his heart. He wanted the world to know He and the people he led were God's treasured possession, a nation favored and distinctive from every other people group on earth.

According to Exodus 33:17, how did God respond to Moses' heartfelt plea?

Now read Exodus 33:18–23. What was Moses request in verse 18?

What do you think Moses meant when he passionately asked God this question?

Moses desired to know God more fully. He wanted to see more of God than he had ever seen before.

The glorious pillar of cloud was right there before him in the tent. God was meeting with Moses as a man meets with his friend. But Moses desired to know God more fully. He wanted to see more of God than he had ever seen before. He wanted to have a greater knowledge of the great "I AM." Moses sought more of His Lord.

Summarize God's response below:

____

____

____

____

The Lord indeed had mercy on and compassion towards His servant Moses by promising to give him a greater revelation of His active presence. Moses would indeed see a miraculous, intimate display of Yahweh's glory.

According to verse 23, what did God say Moses would see when he removed his hand?

____

____

I'd like to suggest that God's phrasing actually illustrates the way we see His active presence manifested today. We don't see God's glorious presence revealed before He acts. Just as Moses only was allowed to see God's back, we only see the after-effects of His glory.

You don't see Him thundering down from heaven before you get the cancer diagnosis. You see the after-effects of His glory when you come through the treatments and hear the words, "cancer free." His work on your wayward son's heart may not be visible to you for years, but you recognize the after-effects of His active presence when your boy quietly walks through the doors of your church sanctuary one Sunday and slips into the seat beside you. You don't see the light of His presence shining in your daughter's dorm room as you fearfully prays for God to somehow supply the funds for her college education. You see the after-effects of His glory as she walks across a stage sporting her cap and gown as she receives her diploma. You don't see God's active presence heading in your direction; you see "His back," the after-effects of our Lord's extraordinary glory.

WEEK SIX **DAY FIVE**

Personal Application

Worship has been our theme this week. Earlier in our lessons we read about the Tabernacle as Moses was presented with the heavenly blue print for this sacred sanctuary. It was a holy structure, and God was specific about the materials used, the dimensions of its components, and even the placement of each piece of furniture. Every aspect of the sanctuary had a purpose and a divinely appointed place.

What do you learn about the tabernacle from Hebrews 8:5?

Look back at your diagram. Today as we peek behind the elaborate, hand-spun tapestries adorning its entrance, we will get a shadowy glimpse of heaven. As a way of closing out our week, rather than using the usual format for our personal application lesson, I'd like to take a tour of God's holy Tabernacle and dig into some Scripture to discover how Jesus is revealed in each piece of furniture within God's holy sanctuary.

Stop for a moment to pray before entering God's holy structure through the pages of your Bible. I can hear God's words to Moses back at the burning bush . . .

> *Take off your sandals, for the place where you are standing is holy ground. (Exodus 3:5b)*

As we enter the courtyard of the Tabernacle, the first structure we encounter is the Altar of Burnt Offering. Label it, and read Leviticus 1:1–8.

As we enter the courtyard of the Tabernacle, the first structure we encounter is the Altar of Burnt Offering.

Look closely at verse 4 below:

He is to lay his hand on the head of the burnt offering, and it will be accepted on his behalf ***to make atonement for him.*** (Emphasis added)

Who would place his hand on the head of an animal and slaughter it for the offering (v. 2)?

What was the purpose of the sacrifice (v. 4)?

In the Old Testament, the word "atonement" means to cover over. But "the secondary meaning of the word is one of reconciliation, or 'at-one-ment'—the bringing together into harmony of those who have been separated.[31] As an Israelite entered the Tabernacle courtyard, he would bring a sheep, ram, or a goat along with him. He would place his hand on the head of that innocent animal and then slaughter it there at the altar to cover over his sin and reconcile himself (temporarily) to God. The blood of the innocent was required to cover over the sin of the guilty.

According to 2 Corinthians 5:18, how did God reconcile us to Himself?

The Altar of Burnt Offering hints of Jesus' atoning sacrifice for our sin on the cross—the innocent whose blood covered over the sin of the guilty. Before moving on with our tour, stop for a moment to thank God for the atoning sacrifice of His Son to cover your sin.

Write your thoughts:

Now move westward, toward the Tent of Meeting where you will encounter the Basin positioned in front of the entrance to the Holy Place. Only priests could enter the Tabernacle's Holy Place.

Now move westward, toward the Tent of Meeting where you will encounter the Basin positioned in front of the entrance to the Holy Place.

We looked at this passage last week, but refresh your memory by reading 1 Peter 2:9–10 and note how you are identified as a believer in Jesus Christ?

As a member of the royal priesthood, you have access to that Holy Place. But before we go inside, we need to stop at the basin which was placed in the courtyard for the priests to wash their hands and feet as a means of purification before entering the Tent of Meeting (Exodus 30:17–21).

Read 1 Corinthians 6:9–11.

My friend, through Christ, you are sanctified, washed clean, and justified. Regardless what sins you have committed, like a priest washing his hands and feet clean in the basin each time he prepared to enter the Holy Place, you can be washed clean each time you confess your sins and allow Jesus to cleanse you anew. Sanctification is an ongoing, continual process.

Interestingly, according to Exodus 38:8, what was used to create the Tabernacle's basin?

The mirrors are a perfect representation of the first step in the sanctification process. We need to take a good look in the mirror, so to speak; make an honest examination of our hearts, our motives and our actions before we are ready to confess our sins and be washed clean, sanctified, and justified afresh before God. Let's take a moment to practice.

Read Psalm 139:1–4 and 23–24 as a prayer and then take a few minutes to confess your sins. Ask God to sanctify you through and through (1 Thessalonians 5:23) and to wash you clean as you take a moment to wash in the basin of His courtyard.

Let us draw near to God with a sincere heart in full assurance of faith, having our hearts sprinkled to cleanse us from a guilty conscience and having our bodies washed with pure water. Let us hold unswervingly to the hope we profess, for he who promised is faithful. (Hebrews 10:22-23 NIV)

Now, let's quietly slip into the Holy Place. The first piece of furniture we encounter is the Table of the Bread of the Presence. Please label it on your diagram. If you recall from our lesson earlier this week, there were twelve loaves of bread kept on the table in the presence of God at all times (Leviticus 24:5–8), one loaf of bread for each of the twelve tribes of Israel. The table and bread reflected God's willingness to fellowship and commune with His people. It was like an invitation to share a meal together as the Israelite elders had done on Mount Sinai. Even when the table was transported during the Israelites' wilderness travels, the bread remained in

Now, let's quietly slip into the Holy Place. The first piece of furniture we encounter is the Table of the Bread of the Presence.

its place on the table (Numbers 4:7–8) from Sabbath to Sabbath and then the loaves were replaced.

Read John 6:32–35.

Who is the bread of God (v. 33)?

____

How did Jesus describe Himself in verse 35? ______________________________

At Jesus' last meal with His disciples, what did Jesus say about the bread according to Matthew 26:26?

____

God has always desired fellowship with His people. So much so, He was willing to come to earth as the "bread of life" to be broken so that we could have eternal fellowship with Him. The Table of the Bread of Presence was a foreshadowing of that day when Jesus, the true bread of God, would give His life for the world.

We need to move on with our tour. Turn from the table and look to your left. Please label the next piece of furniture in the holy place, the Lampstand, with its seven branches and seven oil lamps. It provided the only light for the Holy Place (Exodus 25:37), which was completely covered by a tent of ram skins and the hides of sea cows (Exodus 26:14).

> Turn from the table and look to your left. Let's focus upon the next piece of furniture in the holy place, the Lampstand

How is the Son described in Hebrews 1:3? ______________________________

The Amplified Bible describes Him this way: "He is the sole expression of the glory of God [the Light-being, the out-raying or radiance of the divine]." Jesus also described Himself as the Light of the World (John 8:12). The Lampstand depicts Jesus as that "light-being" of the world.

Now let's focus westward toward the Most Holy Place. In front of the curtain we will find the Altar of Incense. Incense was burned on this altar every morning and every evening when the High priest would light the lamps on the lampstand (Exodus 30:7–8).

To what is prayer compared to Psalm 141:2?

____

How is incense described in Revelation 5:8?

The incense represents the prayers of God's people. Your prayers are precious to God. Take a moment to offer up a little fragrant incense before our Lord. Pray for some of the matters that are burdening you today:

According to Romans 8:34 and Hebrews 7:25 where is Jesus and what is He doing?

Jesus lives. He is seated at the right hand of God and you can rest in the assurance that He is always interceding on your behalf. The Altar of Incense typifies God the Son's prayers to God the Father for all of the saints.

We will end our tour of the Tabernacle here for today. Only the high priest was able to enter the Most Holy Place of God's sacred sanctuary. Later in our study, we will venture behind the beautiful curtain embellished with cherubim that conceals the Most Holy Place. For now, please label the square inside "Ark of the Covenant" and then exit the Tent of Meeting. As you exit the courtyard, take a moment to note what you found most meaningful about your tour today.

Enter his gates with thanksgiving and his courts with praise; give thanks to him and praise his name. (Psalm 100:4)

Week 7

Glorious Aftereffects

WEEK SEVEN DAY ONE

Hungry on Mount Sinai

Moses was there with the Lord forty days and forty nights without eating bread or drinking water.

EXODUS 34:28A

When we last saw Moses he was on Mount Sinai, petitioning God with that famous appeal, "Now show me your glory." Moses was hungry for a greater awareness of God's presence. Our Lord graciously responded by promising to grant his request. God said He would put Moses in the cleft of a rock, cover him with His almighty Hand, and allow His servant to see His "back" after all of His goodness passed by.

> Moses was hungry for a greater awareness of God's presence.

I imagine Moses was eagerly anticipating that moment when God would allow him to indeed see more of His glory. But there was something Moses needed to take care of first. Read Exodus 34:1–4. What did God tell Moses to do before coming back up onto the mountain?

If you recall, God created the first set of tablets Himself. Did you sense a bit of a rebuke in God's directive to Moses? In a fit of anger, Israel's passionate leader had broken the first tablets, which were sacred documents representing God's covenant with His people. Not to mention, those documents had been written by the very finger of God (Exodus 31:18). This time, Moses would have to chisel those stone plaques himself—and he had to do it by morning. I imagine the humbled leader hotfooted it down that mountain and got right to work chiseling and sanding . . . and chiseling and sanding. I doubt he got much sleep and those eighty-year-old muscles were probably screaming for the ancient desert version of IcyHot®. However, Moses showed up on the mountain the next morning with those replacement tablets in his weary, calloused hands. Let's see what happened next.

Read Exodus 34:5-7 out loud and replace "the LORD" with Yahweh as you read.

> Moses' deepest desire was to know God more intimately (Exodus 33:13).

Moses' deepest desire was to know God more intimately (Exodus 33:13). Yahweh graciously responded by granting the desire of His servant's heart. Moses saw a more full expression of God's glory than he had ever seen before. Yahweh proclaimed His name and then went on to list some of His attributes.

In the lists below, check the attributes God mentioned:

___ Compassionate
___ Forgiving
___ Slow to Anger
___ Abounding in Faithfulness
___ Abounding in Love
___ Gracious
___ Jealous
___ Maintaining Love to Thousands

In addition to His gracious nature, God is also a righteous judge and although He delights to show mercy (Micah 7:18), there are times when punishment is the just response. However, I'd like to take a few minutes to clarify the last part of God's statement in the following verse:

. . . maintaining love to thousands, and forgiving wickedness, rebellion and sin. Yet he does not leave the guilty unpunished; he punishes the children and their children for the sin of the fathers to the third and fourth generation. (Exodus 34:7)

Sadly, our sin impacts our children. They will have a natural tendency to repeat the choices of their parents. God often ends up punishing children for the same sins for which He punished their parents. However, we can rest assured, each person is responsible for his or her own sin.

Let's look at some passages in which God provides more clarity about His perspective on personal responsibility and the punishment for sin. To give you some context, many years after the time of Moses, when the Israelites were settled in their promised land, God's people refused to accept responsibility for their behavior. Instead, they blamed their parents and quoted a popular proverb that they felt excused their behavior.

Hold you place in Exodus 34 (We'll return), then read Ezekiel 18:3–5, 9–14, 17–18. Summarize what God had to say regarding generational sin and personal responsibility in these passages:

If you are a parent, Exodus 34:7 should motivate you to seek God for help in overcoming patterns of sin that have been prevalent in your family, perhaps, for generations. Can you think of some behaviors or rebellious tendencies you have picked up from your parents or grandparents? On the line below, write a word (It can be in code!) representing that behavior(s).

Our culture isn't real keen on taking personal responsibility for one's actions, but blaming our parents doesn't give us a divine pass. On the other hand, we are not punished for our parents' sins. Sometimes we endure consequences resulting from their sin, but each person is responsible for his or her own behavior. As believers in Christ, we should be motivated to live in a way that honors God. We have the assurance that we are not condemned (Romans 8:1) and through the power of the Holy Spirit living within us, we have the ability to break patterns of sin that have been part of our family heritage for generations.

Our culture isn't real keen on taking personal responsibility for one's actions, but blaming our parents doesn't give us a divine pass.

Write 2 Corinthians 5:17 on the lines below in your own words:

You are a new creation. The old is gone, and the **new** you can overcome your past. The Lord is compassionate and gracious, slow to anger and abounding in love, but as a parent, you need to do whatever it takes to overcome the patterns of sin in your family. Sin brings consequences. May the Lord never revisit your sins in the lives of your children or your grandchildren. Take a moment to pray for future generations in your family and ask God for the courage and strength to break patterns of sin, not only for your benefit, but also for the good of your ancestors. Write your prayer here:

Now read Exodus 34:8–10.

God would renew His covenant (symbolized by the stone tablets) and He assured Israel's leader that His people would see an awesome display of His glory. God went on to remind Moses of some of laws His people were agreeing to keep.

Read Exodus 34:27–28.

Moses wrote all of those laws down and then the Lord once again wrote the Ten Commandments on the stone tablets His servant had diligently chiseled out of stone. What did Moses do without during his forty days on Mount Sinai with God?

Moses fasted. Fasting was usually observed as a sign of mourning for sin, the objective being to ward off divine wrath or win divine compassion."[32] The Israelites had sinned and broken the covenant before the original tablets were ever delivered. Moses humbly approached God with the new, freshly chiseled plaques, he fasted, and he requested God's divine compassion on behalf of the nation.

I've fasted for a couple days at a time, but I cannot imagine going forty days without food or water. Interestingly, look at Deuteronomy 8:2–3 and note the lesson God taught His people by allowing them to go without food in the desert.

Moses was hungry on Mount Sinai, not only for bread, but for more of God's glory. It appears our humble leader was satisfied by "every word that comes from the mouth of the Lord" and by the greater revelation of His glorious power and character. The Lord met Moses' every need with the manifestation of His active presence revealed that day on Mount Sinai. As we'll see in tomorrow's lesson, Moses was beaming from his experiences atop that mountain.

Moses was hungry on Mount Sinai, not only for bread, but for more of God's glory.

WEEK SEVEN DAY TWO

Radiance Remains

We are not like Moses, who would put a veil over his face to keep the Israelites from gazing at it while the radiance was fading away.

2 CORINTHIANS 3:13

Moses spent forty days and forty nights on Mount Sinai in the presence of God. Israel's leader saw a greater manifestation of God's active presence than he had encountered during any of his previous meetings with his Lord. It must have been an invigorating and humbling experience for Moses as God renewed His covenant with the Israelites, revealed more of His glorious presence, and then, once again carved the Ten Commandments on tablets of stone.

Moses spent forty days and forty nights on Mount Sinai in the presence of God.

As Moses descended Mount Sinai and returned to camp, it was evident to everyone that Moses had an extraordinary forty days on the mountain with God.

Please read Exodus 34:29–32.

What did the Israelites observe when Moses first arrived at the base of Mount Sinai and how did they respond to their leader?

Moses wasn't aware that his face was radiant as he descended the mountain. Can you imagine his surprise when the people scattered and wouldn't go near him? After being reassured, who came to greet Moses (v. 31)?

I sure wish I could have been standing in that huddle as Aaron and the other leaders described Moses' appearance and the humble leader discovered he was reflecting the radiance of his Lord's glory. I can't imagine what words Moses used as he attempted to describe his extraordinary experience at the top of the mountain. After this surreal discussion, Aaron and the community leaders were somehow able to assure the people that Moses was still approachable.

Hold your place at Exodus 34 and then look back at a passage we read last week. How is the radiance around God described in Ezekiel 1:28?

Could it be that Moses' face was also beaming somewhat like a rainbow in the clouds on a rainy day? Whatever it looked like, the passionate leader's face reflected the radiance of God's glorious presence and it was bright enough to frighten the people of Israel.

Now read Exodus 34:33–35.

According to verse 33, what did Moses do after he finished speaking to the Israelites?

When did Moses remove the veil and when did he once again put the veil back over his face?

Let's gain some insight into why Moses began this curious ritual.

What do you learn from 2 Corinthians 3:13 (at the beginning of our lesson) about the reason Moses covered his face with a veil?

As Moses relayed God's commands to the Israelites that day, he somehow became aware that the radiance of God's glory was beginning to fade from his face. Moses conveyed God's message, reassured the people that God was mercifully renewing His covenant with them (despite the embarrassing golden calf incident!), and allowed the Israelites to gaze at the divinely inscribed tablets for the first time. However, as soon as Moses finished talking, he quickly put on a veil so the Israelites would remember their leader with the radiance of God's glorious, active presence all over his face.

As Moses relayed God's commands to the Israelites that day, he somehow became aware that the radiance of God's glory was beginning to fade from his face.

Ladies, Moses wanted God's people to associate him with God's glory. Whenever the passionate servant talked with God, he would remove the veil and bask in His Lord's glorious presence. Beaming with the after-effects of God's glory, Moses then kept that veil off as he returned to camp and relayed God's message. Then, before the radiance of His Lord could fade completely away, he would place the veil back over his face until the next time he entered the Lord's presence.

I'm so moved by Moses' passion, but even more touched by the realization that we, as believer's in Jesus Christ, have the privilege of regularly living out the desire of our zealous protagonist's heart.

Read 2 Corinthians 1:21–22. What is placed in our hearts as believers in Christ?

Now read Romans 8:28–29. What is God's ultimate purpose for you?

When you became a believer in Jesus Christ, God placed His Spirit in your heart and began the process of transforming you into the image of His Son. He uses every experience—pleasant or unpleasant—to mold you and shape you, orchestrating "everything in conformity with the purpose of His will" (Ephesians 1:11) by continually working to transform you more fully into the image of His beloved Son.

Read 2 Corinthians 3:18 below:

And we, who with unveiled faces all reflect the Lord's glory, are being transformed into his likeness with ever-increasing glory, which comes from the Lord, who is the Spirit.

Unlike Moses, who realized the radiance of God's glory was fading from his face shortly after leaving God's presence, as we are transformed more and more into the likeness of our Savior, the after-effects of God's glory increase rather than diminish.

Write our definition of God's glory on the lines below (see page 56).

God's Spirit lives within your heart, molding and transforming you into the likeness of Christ. His work within you is a manifestation of God's active presence in your life. When people around you see the after-effects of God's presence and power through your transformed character, you glorify God (make His active presence visible to others) just as Moses did when he came down from Mount Sinai with the radiance of God's glory all over his face. Rather than fading, however, your radiance grows and you glorify God with "ever-increasing glory."

You, as a believer in Christ, are radiant with the glory of our Lord. Take a moment to thank God for the privilege of glorifying Him to others. Write a prayer of thanksgiving below:

> You, as a believer in Christ, are radiant with the glory of our Lord.

___

___

___

The radiance on Moses' face remained for a time, but then faded. Israel's passionate leader wore a veil in an effort to preserve his association with God's glory. We, however, are not like Moses. Because of the indwelling of the Lord's Holy Spirit in our hearts, we can reflect God's glory with increasing measure as we learn, grow, and change through the transforming work of our dynamically present God. His radiance remains—with ever-increasing glory! May I hear an Amen?

WEEK SEVEN | **DAY THREE**

Blessed Glory

So the cloud of the Lord was over the tabernacle by day, and fire was in the cloud by night, in the sight of all the house of Israel during all their travels.

EXODUS 40:38

After Moses came down from the mountain, it was time to begin crafting the sacred furnishings for the Tabernacle, according to God's precise specifications. Skilled craftsmen created the curtains, carved the furniture, pounded out the bronze basin and molded the golden lampstand. The priestly garments for Aaron and his sons were carefully sewn. Once complete, Moses carefully inspected each individual component.

Read Exodus 39:32–43.

Every element of the sacred sanctuary had been completed and the skilled men brought all of them to Moses. As the meticulous project manager inspected each curtain and furnishing, I imagine he reminisced of his time on the mountain as God relayed His heavenly blueprints. Moses' heart must have been pounding a little more quickly when he finished his inspection and found everything had been completed according to God's instructions.

According to verse 43, what did Moses do for those who had been a part of the construction project for the Tabernacle?

____

____

____

Numbers 6:22–27 records a beautiful blessing pronounced over God's people, which was either the blessing referred to in verse 43, or was said sometime just after Moses' blessing. I've recorded it and substituted Yahweh for "the LORD" to give you a better sense of the powerful affirmation it would have been to God's people. Underline the assurances the Israelites had through this special blessing, carefully written by Yahweh Himself:

Then the LORD said to Moses, "Tell Aaron and his sons to bless the people of Israel with this special blessing:

May [Yahweh] bless you and protect you.
May [Yahweh] smile on you and be gracious to you.
May [Yahweh] show you his favor and give you his peace.

Whenever Aaron and his sons bless the people of Israel in my name,
I myself will bless them." (Numbers 6:22-27 NLT)

God said whenever the priests would bless the people of Israel in His name, He would bless them.

God said whenever the priests would bless the people of Israel in His name, He would bless them. Considering all that had happened in the Israelites' then recent history, why do you think this blessing might have been particularly comforting to them?

Interestingly, two silver amulets "incised with slightly shorter versions of the priestly benediction" were discovered in an excavation of a Jerusalem tomb."[33] I imagine the wearers of those amulets treasured the idea that God would protect them, smile on them, grant them grace and favor, and bestow His peace upon them. What about you? If you had to write an abbreviated from of this blessing on a necklace you could wear around your neck, what aspect of this blessing would you want written?

With the blessing recited, Moses began the work of constructing the sacred sanctuary. Read Exodus 40:1–33 and try to picture Moses in the Tabernacle. Use your diagram if you need some help remembering where each piece of furniture was placed.

What did Moses place inside the Ark of the Covenant (v. 20)?

The Ten Commandments, also called the Testimony, were placed inside the Ark of the Covenant. Now, if you are like me, you wondered why they would be kept in the Ark. The Israelites didn't have access to the Most Holy Place where the Ark was housed. So, what was God's reason for placing the stone tablets there?

In every depiction I've ever seen of these sacred tablets, half of the commands were written on one plaque and the other five were written on the second plaque. However, more recent knowledge of covenant forms suggests the entire list of Ten Commandments was possibly written on each tablet. Ancient covenants were typically written in duplicate, with each party in the covenant maintaining a copy of the agreement. For instance, when two people groups made an agreement, one copy would be maintained by the covenant-god of one group and the second copy would be placed in the sanctuary of the god of the people on whom he was imposing his covenant. In this case, Yahweh was the Covenant-Lord (making the covenant) and also God of Israel (the God of the people on whom He was imposing the covenant). Therefore, it is possible that Yahweh took both copies into His care because the whole care, continuance, and maintenance of the covenant relationship rests with him.[34]

Moses set up the Tabernacle and moved the sacred furnishings carefully into place. As soon as the Most Holy Place was completed, the passionate, law-entrusted leader placed those covenantal documents into the Ark of the Covenant and moved the golden Ark into position behind the shielding curtain. He worked his way from the Tent of Meeting out to the Courtyard, building and measuring as he worked.

How does Exodus 40:33 end? ____

Now read Numbers 7:1–11.

What did Moses do immediately after he finished setting up the Tabernacle (v. 1)?

____

Everything was anointed and then the Israelite leaders brought oxen and carts to be used in the work of the Tabernacle. A leader from each tribe brought an ox and then joined with the leader of another tribe to bring one cart as an offering for the Tabernacle's dedication. Additional contributions were collected from one tribe each day for twelve consecutive days. Let's see what each tribe offered at this celebratory dedication.

Read Numbers 7:12–17 and match the item offered with its purpose:

Silver Plate & Sprinkling Bowl filled with Flour & Oil	Fellowship Offerings
Gold Dish filled with Incense	Altar of Incense (not stated)
1 Young Bull, 1 Ram & 1 Male Lamb	Grain Offerings
1 Male Goat	Sin Offerings
2 Oxen, 5 Rams, 5 Male Goats & 5 Lambs	Burnt Offerings

These gifts were probably treasured possessions, brought to the sanctuary in a loving act of worship from the people of Israel. What did God tell Moses in Numbers 7:4–5?

____

Ladies, God accepts our offerings and recognizes our sacrifices. God's people had sinned and grumbled and had even succumb to worshipping a powerless golden calf, but God mercifully accepted their offerings at His sacred sanctuary. What offerings and sacrifices have you made recently that you want to know God has accepted and will use for His holy purposes?

____

Moses distributed the gifts among the Levites as "each man's work required." The Tabernacle was complete, the priests were in place, and the Levites, who were commissioned to handle all of the daily duties of the Tabernacle, had all they needed to serve God and perform their work. The sanctuary was complete.

Now read Exodus 40:34–38.

What returned to the Israelite camp? ____________

____

____

As God promised, His presence once again went before His people.

Once again, God's active presence was expressed by the familiar cloud by day and fire by night. This time, God's glory was veiled by the elaborate Tabernacle. As God promised, His presence once again went before His people. He guided them, led them through the desert, and made His glory evident to them. When the cloud would lift, it was time to set out and travel to their next destination. When the cloud stopped, it was time to once again set up the Tabernacle and establish a new camp in the wilderness. God blessed them. He protected them, was gracious toward them, showed them favor (after-all, this nation was His people) and I imagine His continual presence among them brought them peace.

To close, read Numbers 7:89 and note what blessing Moses received after he finished the work of constructing the Tabernacle:

____

There, above the cover between the two cherubim that are over the ark of the Testimony, I will meet with you . . . (Exodus 25:22)

Rest assured, God blesses us most by faithfully keeping His Word.

WEEK SEVEN **DAY FOUR**

Led by Glory

At the Lord's command they encamped, and at the Lord's command they set out. They obeyed the Lord's order, in accordance with his command through Moses.

NUMBERS 9:23

It had been about a year since the Israelites had exited Egypt and the entire community celebrated a Passover meal commemorating their deliverance. God's glory filled the Tabernacle and God had begun meeting with Moses at the sacred Ark in His sanctuary. The Levites cared for the holy structure and Aaron served as High Priest. His descendants had been commissioned to minister as priests at God's sanctuary for generations to come.

The cloud's presence over the Tent of Meeting, both day and night, served as a continual reminder that the masses camping in the wilderness were God's people. Begin today by reading Numbers 9:15–23.

How did the Israelites know when to move from one location to another?

Ancient Israel didn't have modern-day technical abilities. There weren't any sound systems or loud speakers. So, rather than have Moses attempt to communicate to the thousands camped around God's Tabernacle, His glorious pillar

> His glorious pillar of cloud communicated the time for departure. Interestingly, God also had Moses establish another means of communicating with the masses.

of cloud communicated the time for departure. Interestingly, God also had Moses establish another means of communicating with the masses.

Read Numbers 10:1–10.

The trumpet calls served several purposes. First, they would signal the tribes to depart in an orderly fashion and were used to summon leaders for meetings at the Tabernacle. Second, they were to be blown as the fighting men went into battle against their enemies. Finally, the trumpets would sound at times of rejoicing during the appointed feasts and festivals.

What assurance did the trumpet calls bring when the Israelites entered battle (v. 9)?

What purpose did the trumpet calls serve at festivals, feasts and during times of offering, (v. 10)?

I'm excited to share some information I found in one of my commentaries about these trumpet calls. Keeping our definition of God's glory in mind, read the excerpt below:

> By blowing the trumpets before battle, Israel expected God's active presence in the battle scene. As in the case of battle, it appears that the blowing of the trumpets was a means of knowing that the people were remembered by the Lord. The trumpets were blown as a [psalm or hymn] to prepare the people for an active confrontation with God.[35]

With the blow of those distinctive trumpet blasts, the entire camp would anticipate a manifestation of God's active presence—in front of them as they traveled in the form of the pillar of cloud or fire, in battle by empowering the soldiers to win, or in the midst of their celebrations by honoring their sacrifices and accepting their acts of worship. In other words, with each trumpet blast, the Israelites expected to be eyewitnesses to God's glory. Isn't that inspiring? From this day forward, I'll think of the Lord whenever I see a silver trumpet and I will pray for a glimpse of His glory when I hear a trumpet blast.

With each trumpet blast, the Israelites expected to be eyewitnesses to God's glory.

After the trumpets were hammered out, it was time for God's people to leave their camp at the base of Mount Sinai.

They had been at that location for about eleven months (Exodus 19:1) and it was now time to move on.

God had an appointed formation in which the twelve tribes of Israel marched during their travels. Read Numbers 10:11–28 and fill in the information below. Try to picture the scene as the Israelites' marched into the desert.

Carrying their tribal banners and traveling by tribe, the procession began as follows:

The Tribe of ____________________ (v. 14)

The Tribe of Issachar (v. 15)

The Tribe of Zebulun (v. 16)

What did the Gershonites and Merarites (Levitical Tribes) carry behind the tribe of Zebulun?

____

The Tribe of ____________________ (v. 18)

The Tribe of Simeon (v. 19)

The Tribe of Gad (v. 20)

The Kohathites (another Levitical Tribe) followed Gad. What did they carry and why would they follow far behind their Levite brothers (v. 21):

____

____

The Tribe of ____________________ (v. 22)

The Tribe of Manasseh (v. 23)

The Tribe of Benjamin (v. 24)

The Tribe of ____________________ (v. 25)

The Tribe of Asher (v. 26)

The Tribe of Naphtali (v. 27)

I imagine the procession was quite an impressive sight on that wilderness horizon as the Israelites marched, each tribe proudly carrying its tribal banner.

As perplexed as I am about certain details God decidedly left out of His Word, I am equally touched by the details He chose to include. Right in the middle of this account of the Israelites setting out from Mount Sinai, God saw fit to include a detail that gives us another glimpse into the family relationships of our central character, Moses.

> As perplexed as I am about certain details God decidedly left out of His Word, I am equally touched by the details He chose to include.

Read Numbers 10:29–32.

Who did Moses encourage to join him on his journey to the Promised Land and what promise did Moses make to help ensure an affirmative response?

____

____

____

____

Perhaps Hobab knew areas of the countryside of which Moses was unfamiliar. Evidently Hobab knew the region well, but considering Moses shepherded sheep in this area for forty years, I would imagine he probably could have navigated and selected a camping area himself. However, Moses appeared to want his brother-in-law with him as he traveled. Family was probably a treasured comfort for Moses. After all, he lived in a tent and traveled from place to place without a stable place to call home.

I remember when our family was looking for a new church home after attending the same church for more than sixteen years. As we visited service after service, we encountered different types of music, a variety of preaching styles, and met many new people. However, without a familiar place to call home, I found myself feeling a bit lonely as we walked through unfamiliar hallways and looked for seats amid strangers. I was thankful to have Mark and our kids to share that experience with me. Family often becomes a comforting constant when we find ourselves in frequently changing territory.

Can you recall a time when the presence of family members was particularly special to you? If so, what were the circumstances?

To conclude our lesson today, read Numbers 10:33–36.

What went before the tribal procession as the Israelites traveled through the desert?

If I had lived during the time of the Exodus, I would have considered it a great privilege to follow Moses. Not only did he speak to the Lord as a man speaks with his friend, but Moses followed God with a continual sense of reverent expectation. Moses knew from experience, God is powerful. He not only knew God was able to accomplish His divine purposes, Moses expected God to do "good things" for the nation he served. I challenge you to live your life with a sense of reverent expectation, just as Moses did. You just might find yourself shouting the words, "Rise up, O Lord!" as you start each new day, determined to be led by His matchless glory.

WEEK SEVEN **DAY FIVE**

Personal Application

Application for Day One

In Day One, we witnessed Moses observing a manifestation of God's glory unlike any he had seen before. To begin today's application lesson, re-read Exodus 33:22–23.

What did God tell Moses he would see as all of His goodness by?

____

Like Moses, God doesn't allow us to see the fullness of His glory, but He does allow us to see "His back"—the after-effects of His active presence at work in our lives. On the lines below, share some of the after-effects of God's glory that have been evident in your life:

> Like Moses, God doesn't allow us to see the fullness of His glory, but He does allow us to see "His back"—the after-effects of His active presence at work in our lives.

____

____

____

What you have just written is evidence that you, like Moses, have been an eyewitness to glory. Take a moment to thank Him for allowing you to see evidence of His loving work in and around you. Write a brief prayer below:

____

____

____

Application for Day Two

As Moses descended Mount Sinai after his extraordinary encounter with God's glory, his face was beaming. Unfortunately, Moses soon discovered the radiance on his face was only temporary. Anxious to be associated with God's glory, our passionate leader covered his face with a veil to "keep the Israelites from gazing at it as the radiance was fading away" (2 Corinthians 3:13). We, on the other hand, are not like Moses. We have the privilege of reflecting the Lord's glory with "ever-increasing glory" (2 Corinthians 3:18).

Let's explore what creates this "radiance" that we experience with "increasing glory." Read the passages below:

***H**usbands, love your wives, just as Christ loved the church and gave Himself up for her to make her holy, cleansing her by the washing with water through the word, and to present her to himself as a radiant church, without stain or wrinkle or any other blemish, but holy and blameless. (Ephesians 5:25-27)*

Husbands, love your wives, just as Christ loved the church. (Ephesians 5:25)

How is the church described? ______________________________

We, as members of the church—which refers to all believers in Christ, not your specific congregation—have our sins covered by the blood of Jesus, but according to these passages, how else are we cleansed?

____

____

Read John 15:3 and 17:17. What do you learn about the correlation between the Word and that ongoing sanctification process we talked about last week?

____

____

Look back at Exodus 34:27–29. What did Moses receive from God before he came down from the mountain with his face radiant?

____

____

God's Word (spoken and written) is truth. Moses was radiant after spending forty days and forty nights on the mountain with God, learning and recording His commands and watching God re-write the Ten Commandments. Jesus' disciples heard, believed, and understood His teachings and their hearts and minds were changed. As a result, the manner in which those men lived their lives was changed. The same is true of us today. As we hear (or read!), believe, and understand God's Word, our hearts and minds are changed. We begin to live our lives differently and the evidence of God's active presence doing His sanctifying work in our lives causes us to be radiant with God's glory.

Application for Day Three

After Moses presented the Ten Commandments on tablets of stone, his next order of business was to construct God's sanctuary. After everything was carefully set into place, God's glory filled the Tabernacle and then the Israelites worshiped the Lord by bringing offerings that were to be used for God's purposes.

After Moses presented the Ten Commandments on tablets of stone, his next order of business was to construct God's sanctuary.

As we talked about last week, where does 1 Corinthians 6:19–20 tell us God's active presence dwells today?

The Israelites brought offerings to God's sanctuary as an act of worship. Please read Romans 12:1 below and underline what we should offer God as a spiritual act of worship:

So here's what I want you to do, God helping you: Take your everyday, ordinary life—your sleeping, eating, going-to-work, and walking-around life—and place it before God as an offering. Embracing what God does for you is the best thing you can do for him. (MSG)

Read Romans 12:1–2 in your Bible. These passages are called cooperative commands. In other words, God does the sanctifying, but we are called to cooperate with Him in His transforming work—that's the offering part. We live in a world that rejects God's commands and continually pressures us to conform to cultural norms. To offer our lives to God, we have to make a conscious effort to honor God with our everyday, ordinary lives. Resisting cultural pressures takes effort and it requires sacrifice. The Israelites offered valued possessions of silver, gold, livestock, and oil for the work of the Tabernacle. What societal norms or cultural pressures do you regularly have to resist in order to offer your ordinary life to God?

Offering your ordinary life to God isn't easy, but the benefit is worth the effort. The more you choose to cooperate with God in the transformation process by spending time in His Word, applying His principles, and resisting cultural pressures, the more radiant you will become. Like we talked about last week, your light will shine more brightly and you will be a greater reflection of God's glory.

The more you choose to cooperate with God in the transformation process by spending time in His Word, applying His principles, and resisting cultural pressures, the more radiant you will become.

Application for Day Four

Moses followed God's instructions and taught the Israelites to obey His commands. The passionate leader also established distinct trumpet calls as a means of communication within the massive traveling nation of Israel and led God's people with a sense of reverent expectation. Moses continually watched for God's active presence at work around him. With each trumpet blast and every movement of the pillar of cloud, Moses anticipated an encounter with God's glory. He lived his life in a continual state of expectation. As I thought about Moses' perspective toward God, I thought of another group of people who lived more than a thousand years later who reacted to Jesus with a sense of expectation.

Read John 6:1–13.

According to verse 11, to whom did the disciples distribute the bread?

____

____

Jesus only had five small barley loaves and two small fish. Yet, about five thousand men sat down on the grassy hillside to receive a meal. Just as Moses anticipated God's power and favor in battle as the priests blew their silver trumpets, these men expected to see Jesus, the greatest manifestation of God's active presence ever encountered by the human race, provide a meal. Those men sat with a sense of reverent expectation.

Sadly, if Scripture points out that the disciples only distributed to those who were seated, that means there were other people on that mountainside who chose not to sit down. They missed a first-hand encounter with God's glory.

What need do you have today? Please don't write down your child's need or your co-worker's prayer request. Save those for another time. On the line below, right a need you personally have today.

____

____

I believe our Lord wants us to live our lives like those men sitting on the grassy mountainside. To close, re-read Numbers 10:35 and use Moses' passionate words as a springboard to a prayer of reverent expectation. Fill in the blank below with your request.

"Rise up, O Lord! May ______________________________

Now to Him who is able to do immeasurably more than all we ask or imagine, according to His power that is at work within us, to Him be glory in the church and in Christ Jesus throughout all generations, for ever and ever! Amen. (Ephesians 3:20–21)

Week 8

Contagious Discontent and Consequences

WEEK EIGHT DAY ONE

Graves of Craving

Therefore the place was named Kibroth Hataavah,
because there they buried the people who had craved other food.

NUMBERS 11:34

We ended Week Seven of our study watching the Israelites departing Mount Sinai with Moses enthusiastically shouting, "Rise up, O Lord!" as the pillar of cloud and Ark of the Covenant took their places at the front of their procession to lead the way. The orderly masses traveled for three days before the pillar of cloud came to rest at a new location. The tribes filed into camp by divisions. While the tribes continued to arrive, the Levites began to set up the Tabernacle. All of the sacred furnishings were set in place, and God's glory once again filled the Most Holy Place. Once the Israelites settled in, it wasn't long before a familiar sound could be heard in the camp.

Please read Numbers 11:1–3. What did the Israelites do as soon as they settled into their new camp and how did the Lord respond?

How did Moses respond to the cries of the people as the Lord's anger literally burned around them (v. 2)?

Moses appears to have cared deeply about the people God had entrusted to his care. He repeatedly interceded on their behalf. (Hold you place in Numbers.) What does James 5:16 say about the prayers of a righteous man?

Prayer is one of the most important acts leaders can do on behalf of their people. Moses cried out to God and the fire, representing His wrath, died down. After witnessing such a tangible expression of God's anger, one would expect a reverent silence to fall upon the camp. Unfortunately, that wasn't the case and Israel's valiant leader began to lose his patience.

Read Numbers 11:4–9.

Who began to crave other food and spread their contagious dissatisfaction throughout the camp?

The "rabble" mentioned here is probably the mixed multitude of non-Israelites who left Egypt with Israel during the Exodus.[36]

Whining and complaining are contagious. When my children were growing up, there was nothing more abrasive to my nervous system than when Brandon and Brianna were both whining at the same time. I would immediately begin searching for some sort of distraction for the two of them before I started whining about their whining. If you have children (or grand-children), what usually happens when one child begins to whine and complain?

The rabble-rousers started craving the food back in Egypt and soon the entire Israelite camp was wailing in protest. God's sweet provision now seemed monotonous and boring (although, it was not any less miraculous). Whether the flakes were ground in a hand mill or crushed in a mortar; cooked in a pot or made into cakes, this group was tired of eating the same food day after day. Their mouths watered at the thought of the fish, which was readily available at the Nile River. The complaints of the "rabble" spread like a disease throughout the entire camp and their abrasive wailing appears to have worn their leader out.

Let's see what happened next. Please read Numbers 11:10–17.

Moses was weary and it was evident in his response. How many rambling, rhetorical questions did Moses ask God in verses 11–13?

What request did Moses make of God in verse 15?

Moses wasn't seeking God's counsel. He was venting his frustrations and God allowed him to rant. Our Lord knows we all have a breaking point and Moses had just about reached it. In modern language, the exasperated leader said, "Just kill me now, Lord!"

Can you recall a time when you, like Moses, wanted to throw in the towel, so to speak, and just give up? If so, did you take your frustrations to God as Moses did, or did you take some other course of action?

Can you recall a time when you, like Moses, wanted to throw in the towel, so to speak, and just give up?

Thankfully, God can handle our frustrations. If we'll go to Him with our complaints (and rambling rhetorical questions), like Moses, God will not strike us down. He knows our limits and He will mercifully respond by either giving us the strength to move forward or providing a level of relief from our burdens. For Moses, God put His Spirit on another seventy leaders who, in addition to the judges that had already been appointed to help him govern, would share the burden of leadership so Moses could stand up under it.

Read Numbers 11:18–23.

Have you ever noticed that it is difficult to believe God's Word when you are exhausted and discouraged? How have you seen evidence of that fact in your attitude during trying circumstances?

Moses had seen manifestation after manifestation of God's dynamic presence. He knew God was powerful enough to accomplish whatever the situation required. He had witnessed the ten life-altering plagues in Egypt. He was well aware the Lord's arm is never too short. However, Moses was worn out, exhausted, and he urgently needed the support of those additional seventy leaders. His faith was waning under the pressure of His growing responsibilities.

> Moses had seen manifestation after manifestation of God's dynamic presence.

Read Numbers 11:24–30.

What did the seventy elders do after the Lord put His Spirit on them (v. 25)?

The Hebrew word translated "prophesied" in this passage is ***naba*** and it means "to prophesy, i.e. speak (or sing) by inspiration in prediction or simple discourse"(***Strong's Concordance***). The men could have been praising God through song, declaring some of God's decrees, or maybe even telling the Israelites of God's intentions. Whatever they were doing, it was inspired by the Spirit and they only did it once, probably to authenticate themselves to the Israelite community.

Why do you think Joshua, Moses' aide, was so troubled by the fact Eldad and Medad were also prophesying in the camp?

How did Moses respond?

Okay, I laughed as I read Moses' response. In essence, he said, "Are you kidding me? Don't be jealous on my behalf! The more the merrier. I wish everyone could be a prophet and I didn't have to do this job!" Joshua was concerned these men had a rogue operation going here, but Moses was just thrilled to have some help. With the elders established and validated, Moses probably breathed a sigh of relief as his newly identified leadership team returned with him to the wailing bunch of grumblers back in the camp.

As for the Israelites, God may be slow to anger, but His wrath was forthcoming. The next scene is another one of those passages that we often find difficult to read. We want to focus upon God's grace and mercy as New Testament believers. Thankfully, as such, we live under the protection of Jesus' blood every day. However, in order to truly appreciate the depth of God's merciful provision through Jesus' death on the cross, we must accept the reality of His wrath.

> As for the Israelites, God may be slow to anger, but His wrath was forthcoming.

Ask God to thicken your spiritual skin as you read Numbers 11:31–35.

The Lord mustered up a wind over the sea and drove quail over the camp, low enough to the ground so the Israelites could easily gather them up. The birds were flying around everywhere as far as the eye could see. For two days, the people gathered quail. An homer is a donkey load[37] and "no one gathered less than ten"(v. 32). However, according to verse 33, what happened to the people who craved other food?

Once the rest of the Israelites recovered from the shock of what happened to their neighbors, that quail probably didn't look as appetizing. But I imagine they ate it for the next month until they loathed it, just as the Lord said they would.

What name did the people give that place in the desert? ______________________

The name means, Graves of Craving.[38] As the Israelites dug graves for their traveling companions, I would guess each handful of desert sand was a vivid reminder that the cravings for the indulgences of their past could very well become their own demise.

God had delivered them, protected them, and brought them on eagle's wings to Himself. He had faithfully given them manna to eat and demonstrated His ability to deliver drinkable water when needed. His mighty arm was always able to meet their needs, but to make it to the Promised Land, the Israelites would have to stop craving what they had left behind in Egypt.

WEEK EIGHT | **DAY TWO**

Sibling Rivalry

"Has the Lord spoken only through Moses?" they asked.
"Hasn't he also spoken through us?" And the Lord heard this.

Numbers 12:2

As we closed yesterday's discussion, the Israelites had just finished digging graves for some of their fellow travelers who had craved meat and pushed Moses to the edge of his limits with their complaining. In our lesson today, Moses encounters further opposition. This time, the criticism originates closer to home and the accusations are much more personal in nature.

Begin today by reading Numbers 12:1–16. According to verse 1, what was the issue that prompted Miriam and Aaron to speak against Moses?

As we closed yesterday's discussion, the Israelites had just finished digging graves for some of their fellow travelers

---

Scripture doesn't make it clear what "Cushite wife" Miriam and Aaron were referring to, but there are a few possibilities. Perhaps Zipporah had passed away and Moses took on a new, Cushite wife at this point in the journey. Some speculate that Zipporah, herself, could have been a Cushite. However, she was the daughter of a Midian priest and probably would be called a Midianite. Besides, had Miriam and Aaron been upset over Moses' marriage to Zipporah, it seems like this issue would have been brought up sometime earlier. Interestingly, the Jewish historian, Josephus, recorded a story about Moses' life in Egypt that might provide a plausible explanation for this "Cushite wife":

> Tharbis was the daughter of the king of the Ethiopians: she happened to see Moses as he led the [Egyptian] army near the walls, and fought with great courage; and . . . she fell deeply in love with him; and upon the prevalency of that passion, sent to him the most faithful of all her servants to discourse with him about their marriage. He thereupon accepted the offer, on condition she would procure the delivering up of the city; and gave her the assurance of an oath to take her to be his wife; and that when he had once taken possession of the city, he would not break his oath to her. No sooner was the agreement made, but it took effect immediately; and when Moses had cut off the Ethiopians, he gave thanks to God, and consummated his marriage, and led the Egyptians back to their own land.[39]

Cush "was the 'Ethiopia' of classical writers and is present-day Sudan."[40] Could it be that this woman wasn't around when Moses left Egypt, but as word of all God had done through the former Egyptian prince continued to spread throughout the region, this "Cushite wife" suddenly appeared on the scene at Hazeroth?

Could Moses have married Zipporah while technically still married to this daughter of the Ethiopian king? Whether past or present, this circumstance appears to have deemed Moses an unworthy servant in the eyes of Miriam and Aaron.

Being deemed unqualified for service based upon past decisions is a scenario that probably hits close to home for some of us. I, for one, can be overcome with a sense of unworthiness whenever someone asks me about my education. As a senior in high school, my family life was less than stable and having my college education paid for by my parents was not an option. Rather than apply for grants or student loans, I learned some administrative skills and charged into the workforce, determined to prove that I didn't need a college education or assistance from anyone in order to succeed. The road was bumpy and lonely, and sometimes a bit frightening. I somehow managed to survive on a steady diet of green beans and popcorn while working three jobs on my quest to prove my independence. Needless to say, I was humbled along the way as many compassionate people reached out to assist me and generously offered me career opportunities for which I shouldn't have been qualified. I eventually recognized the obstacles my lack of education presented and I enrolled in night classes at my local community college. However, after I got married and then had children, I stopped attending classes and never did finish working on that degree. As I write this, I am keenly aware that I am unqualified to write the study that you have in your hands. Yet, despite all of my weaknesses and my lack of education, God still called me to this work. I'll never understand it, but my service is a constant reminder that God is merciful and His grace is sufficient.

As I write this, I am keenly aware that I am unqualified to write the study that you have in your hands. Yet, despite all of my weaknesses and my lack of education, God still called me to this work.

Read 1 Corinthians 1:26–31 and note the reason God often chooses to use unqualified, unimpressive people to accomplish His work:

You see, when God uses unimpressive, perhaps even unqualified people (from a human viewpoint) to accomplish His divine work, the world sees a manifestation of God's active presence and they come to a greater understanding of His merciful nature and His indisputable power. People become eyewitnesses to His glory when there is no one in which to boast other than the Lord.

People become eyewitnesses to His glory when there is no one in which to boast other than the Lord.

Miriam and Aaron used the fact that Moses had a Cushite wife as a reason to dispute his qualifications for leadership. They might have been technically correct, but Moses was God's chosen servant and He was displeased when the pair spoke against their leader and revealed the envy that had apparently been brewing in their subordinate hearts.

What questions did Miriam and Aaron ask in Numbers 12:2?

Envy is "a feeling of resentment and jealousy over the possessions, achievements, etc., of another; a desire for something belonging to another."[41] ***Webster's*** lists greed and covetousness as synonyms for envy.

Look back at Exodus 20:17. What was the tenth Commandment that Miriam and Aaron heard God speak from Mount Sinai?

As Miriam and Aaron raised the objection over Moses' Cushite wife, the siblings not only revealed their obvious resentment, they made it clear they coveted Moses' position.

Read the following passages and underline the warnings they contain about the dangers of envy:

Resentment kills a fool, and envy slays the simple. (Job 5:2)

A heart at peace gives life to the body, but envy rots the bones. (Proverbs 14:30)

But if you harbor bitter envy and selfish ambition in your hearts, do not boast about it or deny the truth. Such "wisdom" does not come down from heaven but is earthly, unspiritual, of the devil. For where you have envy and selfish ambition, there you find disorder and every evil practice. (James 3:16)

Envy eats away at the person feeling it and leads to gossip, slander, and mean spirited assaults on a person's character. Envy spreads like a cancer to other people, causing disorder, strife, and downright evil behavior.

What punishment was Miriam given as the cloud lifted from the entrance of the Tent of Meeting (Numbers 12:10)?

Aaron had a history of being easily influenced (Let's not forget that he was the one who cast the golden calf). Aaron appears to have zealously joined Miriam's charge, but the fact God chose to strike Miriam with leprosy and not Aaron, suggests she was the one who first spoke against Moses. The infectious skin disease likely began with brownish-red spots that eventually erupted into ulcers and resulted in the loss of tissue.[42] I can't help but wonder if God chose this particular punishment as a painful visual reminder of the damage that could be caused by Miriam's envy driven assault on her brother.

How did Moses respond to his sister's punishment (Numbers 12:13)?

There will be times when you, as God's servant, will encounter attacks that are fueled by unity-killing, bone-rotting envy. I've learned the hard way that, like Moses, it is best not to try to defend yourself from attacks regarding your ministry qualifications. Let's face it, none of us would quality to serve our Lord if it weren't for His unfathomable mercy. If He has called you to a task, regardless how unqualified you may be, it would be disobedience not to serve as God directs. The Lord is a warrior (Exodus 15:3). He will fight for you; you need only to be still (Exodus 14:14). Follow Moses' example. When a brother or sister in Christ falls prey to sibling rivalry, pray for restoration, and like Moses, be around to embrace her should she ever find the courage to humbly return to your camp.

There will be times when you, as God's servant, will encounter attacks that are fueled by unity-killing, bone-rotting envy.

WEEK EIGHT DAY THREE

Abundant Fruit and an Enormous Problem

They gave Moses this account: "We went into the land to which you sent us, and it does flow with milk and honey! Here is its fruit. But the people who live there are powerful, and the cities are fortified and very large. We even saw descendants of Anak there."

NUMBERS 13:27-28

After seven excruciating days of leprosy-driven isolation, Miriam returned to the Israelite camp restored to health. The familiar pillar of cloud awaited her return, and then Israel made a difficult, 150 mile trek through rugged terrain to the Desert of Paran. Here in Day Three, we will envision the Israelites getting their first glimpse of the Promised Land. It was a place their people had talked about for generations and most of them had probably dreamed about their entire lives.

Here in Day Three, we will envision the Israelites getting their first glimpse of the Promised Land.

Read Numbers 13:1–16 and fill in the blanks below with the names of the tribal leaders who were chosen to scope out the "good and spacious land that was flowing with milk and honey".

The tribe of Reuben:	________ (v. 4)	The tribe of Ephraim:	________ (v. 10)
The tribe of Simeon:	________ (v. 5)	The tribe of Benjamin:	________ (v. 11)
The tribe of Judah:	________ (v. 6)	The tribe of Zebulun:	________ (v. 12)
The tribe of Issachar:	________ (v. 7)	The tribe of Manasseh:	________ (v. 13)

The tribe of Dan: ________ (v. 8) The tribe of Naphtali: ________ (v. 14)

The tribe of Asher: ________ (v. 9) The tribe of Gad: ________ (v. 15)

According to verse 16, what name did Moses give Hoshea, son of Nun from the tribe of Ephraim?

____

Hoshea was none other than Moses' trusted aide, Joshua, who led the battle against the Amalekites and traveled with Moses to the top of Mount Sinai when he received the stone tablets inscribed with the Ten Commandments. It makes sense Moses would have chosen his faithful sidekick for this all important mission.

Now read Numbers 13:17–25.

To get a little more information about this exploratory effort, read Deuteronomy 1:19–25.

According to verse 22, whose idea was it to send spies to assess the situation in Canaan?

____

There seems to have been some hesitation among the people when Moses encouraged them to do as God instructed and go take possession of the land. They gathered together and suggested Moses send a group of men ahead of them to determine the best route and see what types of towns they would encounter in the battle. Although the Lord certainly knew the best route and was well aware of exactly what was in store for His people once they arrived, God appears to have agreed to the scouting mission (Numbers 13:1–2). However, look back at Numbers 13:18–20, and note the information Moses asked the spies to obtain:

____

____

____

Before we move forward with the rest of the lesson, hold your place in Numbers (we will read more from these passages), and look up the verses listed below. Note the information God had already provided to Moses and His people about the Promised Land and their ability to take possession of it:

Exodus 3:7–8: ____

Exodus 23:23: ______________________________

Exodus 23:31: ______________________________

God said the land was good and spacious, flowing with milk and honey. He promised to give it as a possession to Abraham's descendants and guaranteed it with a one-sided covenant (Genesis 15). The Lord said He would send an angel ahead of his people to wipe out the current inhabitants of Canaan and those people would be handed over to Israel.

God said the land was good and spacious, flowing with milk and honey.

God agreed to allow the spies to assess the best point of entry. After our discussion in Day Three, I want to be careful what I say about Moses, but might I suggest he got a little carried away with his instructions? In his attempt to gather detailed information, is it possible he inadvertently planted a few seeds of doubt in the minds of his tribal leaders? Did God ever suggest His people take soil samples? Moses should have known the land was "good." God said it was.

According to verse Numbers 13:20, what specific request did Moses make of the spies?

____

With their long list of information to gather, the twelve spies went up through the land and kept on traveling and making notes until they only had one final item left to check off their list—the ripe grapes their leader had requested. I imagine as they sought out the best fruit in the land, the spies were told to go to the Valley of Eshcol, which "even today is famous for its grapes"[43].

According to Numbers 13:22, whom did the spies encounter when they passed through Hebron on their way to gather these ripe grapes for Moses?

____

"Hebron was the home of the Anakites, which was a tribe of giants.[44]" Let's see what happened as a result of Moses' request that the spies "do their best" to bring back a sampling of fresh fruit.

Read Numbers 13:26–33.

What was Caleb's assessment of the situation (v. 30)?

____

WEEK EIGHT

What report did the ten spies spread among the Israelites? (vv. 32–33)?

As the Israelites talked of choosing a new leader and returning to Egypt, they were plotting to abandon their covenant relationship with God.

That fruit may have been exceptional, but the spies couldn't get the Anakites off their minds. Sadly, the all familiar grumbling began to once again spread throughout the camp.

Please read Numbers 14:1–9.

The Hebrew word translated, "rebel" in verse 9 is ***marad.*** The word implies covenant obligations and indicates an attempt to break a covenant relationship.[45] As the Israelites talked of choosing a new leader and returning to Egypt, they were plotting to abandon their covenant relationship with God. The words sparked a dramatic scene. Moses and Aaron fell face-down in front of the whole assembly. Joshua and Caleb tore their clothes and begged the Israelites to come to their senses. Sadly, they didn't.

Read Numbers 14:10. How did the Israelites respond?

The Israelites should have been the ones falling face-down and tearing their clothes as the glory of the Lord began to shine brightly in the cloud above the Tent of Meeting. Had the Israelites forgotten that Yaweh was among them? Moses had probably meant well. Maybe he thought details of the good and spacious land would build the people's faith. Perhaps he thought a little fresh fruit from the land of promise might inspire the crowds. The well-intentioned leader probably wondered how that abundant cluster of grapes could have led to such an enormous problem.

We will end our lesson here for now, but in Day Four we will witness the dramatic conclusion to these history-altering events at Kadesh in the Desert of Paran.

WEEK EIGHT | **DAY FOUR**

Sentenced to Wander

For forty years—one year for each of the forty days you explored the land—you will suffer for your sins and know what it is like to have me against you.

NUMBERS 14:34

In our last episode (It felt like it, didn't it?), the spies returned from Canaan with good fruit and a bad report. Overcome by fear and doubt, the Israelites plotted to select a new leader, abandon their covenant relationship with God, and return to Egypt. Moses and Aaron fell prostrate before the Lord, and Joshua and Caleb tore their clothes in grief as they pleaded with the Israelites not to rebel against Yahweh. The Israelites refused to listen and even discussed stoning their leaders. The day ended with an ominous manifestation of God's glory appearing above the Tent of Meeting.

Our saga continues with a harsh reproof from the Lord. Pay close attention as you read Day Four. These rebellious events led to the famous forty-year wandering in the desert that is often referred to throughout Scripture.

Let's begin with a little review. Read Numbers 14:1–12.

According to verse 3, what did the Israelites say was going to happen if they tried to take possession of the Promised Land?

What did they feel would be in their best interests (v. 4)?

Despite all that God had done and all of the miraculous displays of His active presence among them, the Israelites refused to believe God had their best interests at heart and would keep His promises to them.

What did God threaten to do, and what alternative plan did He mention to Moses (v. 12)?

I can't help but wonder if this offer of starting a new nation made up only of Moses' descendants was a test for our humble leader. A lesser man might think it sounded pretty exciting to one day have a nation comprised solely of Moses-ites living in the Promised Land under God's blessing and favor.

If the Lord's offer was a test, Moses passed. Read Numbers 14:13–19 and summarize Moses' focus in your own words:

Moses wasn't focused on making his own name great. God's chosen leader wanted the world to know about the strength, the mercy and the love Yahweh had for His covenant people. Other nations were watching what happened to the Israelites. Remember the altar Moses built and gave the name, "The Lord Is My Banner"? Those words weren't half-heartedly written during a fleeting moment of passionate worship. Moses believed the Israelites would be a testimony of God's faithfulness to the other nations of the world. Moses pleaded with God to forgive His people in accordance with His merciful nature.

Remember the altar Moses built and gave the name, "The Lord Is My Banner"? Those words weren't half-heartedly written during a fleeting moment of passionate worship.

Please read Numbers 14:20–25. How did the Lord respond to Moses' prayers?

Read the passage below and circle the condition upon which God hears us and grants what we ask of him in prayer:

This is the confidence we have in approaching God: that if we ask anything according to his will, he hears us. And if we know that he hears us—whatever we ask—we know that we have what we asked of him. (1 John 5:14–15)

The Lord honored the prayers of His righteous man of God, so we can rest assured Moses' request was in accordance with God's will and purposes. The Lord agreed to forgive the Israelites. He assured Moses that His glory would indeed fill the whole earth, but this grumbling bunch would not be the ones who would inherit the land of promise. They had been set free from Egypt, but, sadly, their hearts were still entrenched in the "iron-smelting furnace" they said they wanted to leave.

The Lord honored the prayers of His righteous man of God, so we can rest assured Moses' request was in accordance with God's will and purposes.

Read Numbers 14:26–38.

My eyes watered as I read those passages. The entire generation that had been enslaved in Egypt would slowly die off in the desert. They would never see the land they'd dreamed of possessing. In addition, their children would wander and shepherd their flocks in the desert wilderness for the next forty years until every last one of the men twenty years old or older died in the wilderness.

According to verse 34, what was the reason for this particular time frame?

Interestingly, how long was Moses a shepherd in Midian? (See Acts 7:30 if you don't remember.)

Just as Moses was prepared for his service to God during his forty years of shepherding in Midian, the nation of Israel would be refined and prepared to take possession of their Promised Land through their forty years as wandering shepherds. Could it be that the young Israelites who would wander around the desert completely dependent upon God for the next forty years would develop a greater hunger for a place to call home? Regardless the reasons God had for making this decision, God told Moses to have His people turn away from the Promised Land and head back toward the desert along the route to the Red Sea.

Let's see how the Israelites responded to the news. Read Numbers 14:39–45.

What did the Israelites attempt to do? ________________

Faced with living out the rest of their days wandering around in the desert without adequate water and eating the monotonous manna, the Israelites suddenly recognized the error of their ways. Sadly, it was too late for a change of heart.

Read Deuteronomy 1:40–46.

What did the Israelites do after they were defeated by the Amorites and returned to the Israelite camp (v. 45)?

____

God had forgiven these people, but sometimes, even though an offense had been forgiven, the consequences remain. Regardless how long the Israelites pleaded with God and wept over their circumstances, their request was not according to God's will and He was not going to change His mind.

The Israelites may have been fearful, but their initial unwillingness to fight for their Promised Land was still an act of willful disobedience. They wanted to witness God's glory. They desired God's blessings. But when the time came to act on the faith they professed to have, they disobediently refused to face what they perceived to be a difficult battle. As a result, the Israelites allowed their fear of some giants to steal their Promised Land.

Consider the life that awaited them in Canaan. What blessings do you think the Israelites forfeited because of their fear and willful disobedience?

____

____

At the edge of their Promised Land, the Israelite nation was sentenced to wander in the desert for another forty years. They had been unwilling to risk loss in order to follow God and trust in His Word. As a result, they missed an opportunity that would never come their way again. Only their children would one day be given the chance to take possession of the long awaited Promised Land. It was a sad ending to a long, treacherous journey.

They had been unwilling to risk loss in order to follow God and trust in His Word. As a result, they missed an opportunity that would never come their way again.

WEEK EIGHT | DAY FIVE

Personal Application

Application for Day One

In Day One this week, the mixed multitude traveling with the Israelites started craving the luxuries and comforts of Egypt. Their dissatisfaction spread like a disease, and soon the entire Israelite nation was wailing at the entrances to their tents. Even though conditions back in the "iron-smelting furnace" had been miserable, when the people faced new obstacles and hardships, they began to romanticize their time in Egypt.

Sometimes desert walks have a tendency to stir up cravings for days past—the respect former accomplishments or circumstances afforded us, or the luxuries we once enjoyed. As followers of Christ, it is not uncommon for God to humble us by stripping away some pride-inspiring titles or luxurious comforts (at least for a period of time), so we will rely more heavily upon our Lord.

As followers of Christ, it is not uncommon for God to humble us by stripping away some pride-inspiring titles or luxurious comforts

Whether you have followed God for years or only for a few months, has He ever prompted you to leave behind something you once considered precious or comforting? If so, explain:

When I think of someone leaving behind that which is pride inspiring or praise worthy, I think of the apostle Paul. Read Philippians 3:4–6 and list all of the pride-inspiring accomplishments Paul (formerly named Saul) had on his pre-Christian resume:

Now read Philippians 3:7–14. What did Paul consider to be like rubbish compared to the privilege of knowing Christ and following Him.

Summarize verses 13–14 in your own words below:

As you seek to follow our Lord, ask God to give you such joy in His presence that, like Paul, you are able to forget anything your walk with Him requires you to leave behind. Ask Him to make His presence so evident to you that even when you have to trek through barren deserts seasons of life, His glory will satisfy you more than any creature comforts or accolades the world can offer.

Ask God to give you such joy in His presence that, like Paul, you are able to forget anything your walk with Him requires you to leave behind.

Application for Day Two

When you are doing your best to follow God and serve Him faithfully, there is nothing more discouraging than mutiny among your most trusted and treasured ministry companions. Moses had already been near his breaking point over the grumbling and complaining of the masses. When his siblings questioned his qualifications over a decision he probably made many years earlier, I imagine Moses wanted to just quietly hand his staff back to God and set up a small, obscure tent on the outskirts of camp.

Is there a decision or course of action you took some time in your past that, if brought up, might make you appear unqualified to serve God in your church or ministry? If so, briefly explain: (You can write in code, if you like.)

Thankfully, there is no condemnation for those who are in Christ (Romans 8:1). We are new creations and regardless what has happened in the past, we simply need to do our best to faithfully serve and honor God in our present. Thankfully, you don't have to be perfect to serve our Lord. As a matter of fact, He is often most glorified when He chooses to work through the least likely among us.

Application for Day Three

Have you ever allowed perceived obstacles to keep you from following God into new territory? If so, like the Israelites, you may have missed a one-time opportunity to not only witness a manifestation of God's active presence, but also to gain a greater understanding of His power and character.

Have you ever allowed perceived obstacles to keep you from following God into new territory?

Look back at Philippians 3:10. What did the apostle Paul say was his primary goal?

Read the beginning of this passage from the Amplified Bible below:

[For my determined purpose is] that I may know Him [that I may progressively become more deeply and intimately acquainted with Him, perceiving and recognizing and understanding the wonders of His Person more strongly and more clearly], . . .

What a beautiful mission statement for a follower of Christ. To know our Lord with that kind of depth, we have to be willing to follow him wherever He leads. That may mean facing frightening or seemingly impossible obstacles. However, God's glory is most evident when we are most dependent upon His power. We become more deeply and intimately acquainted with Him, perceiving and recognizing and understanding the wonders of His Person more strongly and more clearly. I think that beats safe and comfortable any day.

WEEK EIGHT

Application for Day Four

The Israelites were sentenced to wander for another forty years.

Read Deuteronomy 1:26–36. What plea did Moses make when the Israelites were afraid to fight for their Promised Land (vv. 29–30)?

God's people had seen all the wonders He had performed in Egypt. They saw the pillar of cloud by day and the column of fire at night. They heard God's voice thunder down from Mount Sinai. The Lord's discipline may have seemed harsh, but His nation was weak and unstable and rebellious. Before they were ready to fight giants, they needed to learn to stop fighting God.

Let's skip ahead thirty-eight years in Israelite history. Read Deuteronomy 2:14–16 below and underline the description of the generation of men who died in the desert:

Thirty-eight years passed from the time we left Kadesh Barnea until we crossed the Zered Valley. By then, that entire generation of fighting men had perished from the camp, as the Lord had sworn to them. The Lord's hand was against them until he had completely eliminated them from the camp. Now when the last of these fighting men among the people had died. . . .

How submissive are you to God's plans and purposes? Are you willing to risk facing giants in order to follow God wherever and whenever He leads? Or, like the Israelites, is there a fighting woman inside you that God's discipline needs to remove in order for you to follow Him wholeheartedly like Caleb did? Spend a few moments in prayer and answer those questions silently, just between you and God. His discipline is sometimes painful, but it is always for the greater good.

How submissive are you to God's plans and purposes?

For our earthly fathers disciplined us for a few years, doing the best they knew how. But God's discipline is always good for us, so that we might share in his holiness. No discipline is enjoyable while it is happening—it's painful! But afterward there will be a peaceful harvest of right living for those who are trained in this way. (Hebrews 12:10–11 NLT)

Week 9

Days of Wandering

WEEK NINE DAY ONE

Relative Revolt

They came as a group to oppose Moses and Aaron and said to them, "You have gone too far! The whole community is holy, every one of them, and the Lord is with them. Why then do you set yourselves above the Lord's assembly?"

NUMBERS 16:3

As we learned last week, the Israelites stood at the entrance to their Promised Land, and the Lord told them to turn back and return to the desert. They were sentenced to wander for another forty years—one year for each of the forty days the spies had explored Canaan before bringing back a bad report.

In our Week Nine studies , we will look at some key events from those forty years of desert wandering. Unfortunately, not only were God's people punished with further hardships and struggles, their leader, Moses, was forced to endure four more decades of whining, complaining, and moments of outright rebellion, such as the events we will study today.

Begin by reading Numbers 16:1–3.

Before we get into the heart of this incident, let's get a little more information about Korah. Verse 1 tells us he was from the tribe of Levi.

Hold your place in Numbers, then turn back to Exodus 6:16–21 and fill in the blanks in Korah's family tree:

> In our Week Nine studies , we will look at some key events from those forty years of desert wandering.

LEVI

Gershon **Kohath** Merari

Amram ______________ Hebron Uzziel

Aaron ______________

______________ Nepheg Zicri

What was the relationship between Moses and Korah? ______________

Moses once again faced opposition from a close family member. Korah teamed up with a group of men from the Reubenite tribe and stirred up a revolt. According to Numbers 16:2, what was significant about the 250 men who joined this uprising?

____

Upon what argument did the group base their disrespectful rebellion (v. 3)?

____

Sounds remotely familiar, doesn't it? Miriam and Aaron made similar claims when they said, "Has the Lord spoken only through Moses? Hasn't he also spoken through us?" (Numbers 12:2). What was Miriam's punishment for spearheading that envy-driven attack on her brother's leadership? (Look back at Numbers 12:10 if you don't remember.)

____

It appears Korah hadn't paid much attention to his cousin's previous predicament. As sometimes happens with close family, Korah didn't seem too impressed by Moses or Aaron, and was indignant over the fact they were elevated to positions of authority over the rest of the Israelites.

According to Numbers 4:4, 15, what work were the Kohathites (including Korah and his sons) commissioned to do for the Tent of Meeting?

What were they specifically instructed not to touch (15)? ____________

The Kohathites were restricted from touching the holy furnishings. They were simply instructed to carry them from one location to the next. However, Aaron's descendants, also part of the Kohathite clan, were stationed as priests. They were not only allowed to touch the holy furnishings, but ministered using the holy things in the Tent of Meeting. As high priest, Aaron also had the distinct privilege of venturing behind the dividing curtain and entering the Most Holy Place where God's presence dwelled above the Ark. Moses, also part of the same clan, spoke with God as a man speaks with his friend (Exodus 33:11). Once again, envy-fueled resentment appears to have spurred a family member's assault on Moses' God ordained place "above the Lord's assembly."

> Korah was angry that his cousins were able to touch the holy accessories and use the sacred furnishings in the Tent of Meeting.

Korah was angry that his cousins were able to touch the holy accessories and use the sacred furnishings in the Tent of Meeting. He was determined to prove he was just as holy as his cousins. Korah failed to recognize that God placed these men in their positions of leadership. However, even Aaron and his sons had set rules and regulations for entering God's presence. As a matter of fact, two of Aaron's own sons lost their lives (Leviticus 10:1–2) when they approached God in an unauthorized manner.

Please read Leviticus 16:1–13.

Summarize the requirements Aaron (as the high priest) had to go through in order to be considered holy enough to go behind the dividing curtain into the Lord's presence.

According to verses 12–13, what was the purpose of the censer full of burning coals and the fragrant incense?

WEEK NINE

Moses must have had this ritual in mind as he responded to Korah's accusations. Please read Numbers 16:4–11.

What did Moses tell them to do in order to confirm that they were indeed holy (vv. 6–7)?

Against whom did Moses say these men were banding together (v. 11)?

Read Numbers 16:12–15.

I imagine the veins in Moses' elderly neck were bulging as Dathan and Abiram disrespectfully refused to come when summoned to the Tabernacle. The pair mocked Moses, used God's description of the Promised Land to describe Egypt, and blamed Moses for making them wander in the desert. They even had the audacity to imply Moses was trying to blind the people to his real motives.

Hold your place in Numbers 16 and turn to Romans 13:1–2. Who establishes earthly authorities, and what happens to those who rebel against them?

Moses was God's established leader, and Aaron and his sons were God's designated priests. Our humble protagonist had lost his patience, and God's judgment was about to fall in dramatic fashion. Excuse the pun, but Korah was playing with fire and he was about to get burned.

Moses was God's established leader, and Aaron and his sons were God's designated priests.

Read Numbers 16:16–40.

What happened to Korah and his followers as a result of their rebellion and disrespect for God's chosen leaders?

I am so saddened to read that the families, including little ones, were swallowed up along with these rebellious men. Ladies, Scripture tells us we are subject to our husbands, and we should be supporters of them. However, when those women heard Moses telling the assembly to back away from their husbands' tents or they would be swept away because of their sins, I can't imagine why they didn't they grab their children and move away from the tents. We should never follow authorities into rebellion against God.

Did you notice Korah's family was nowhere to be found? Korah's family appears to have distanced themselves from Korah's rebellion. In fact, Korah's sons went on to have many descendants. They were counted among the Israelites during a census that was taken after their forty-years of wandering in the desert (Numbers 26:58).

At God's command, Aaron's son, Eleazar, pulled the 250 censers from the smoldering remains around the Tabernacle and hammered them into bronze sheets. According to Numbers 16:40, what were the Israelites to remember whenever they saw the bronze sheets overlaying the altar?

Korah allowed envy to fuel a rebellious revolt, and everyone who stood with him was wiped off the face of the earth that day in the desert.

Korah allowed envy to fuel a rebellious revolt, and everyone who stood with him was wiped off the face of the earth that day in the desert. All that remained in the smoldering ruins were the censers Eleazer hammered out flat and laid upon the Altar of Burnt Offering. Each bronze sheet reminded the Israelites of the consequences for usurping God's established authorities.

WEEK NINE

WEEK NINE | DAY TWO

Blossoming Gifts

I am giving you the service of the priesthood as a gift.

NUMBERS 18:7

After the horrific scene at the assembly we observed yesterday, one would expect the sun to rise over the desert horizon to a more agreeable crowd. Unfortunately, those "stiff-necked" Israelites (Exodus 33:5) just could not seem to lift their gaze heavenward. Instead, they continued to focus their eyes (and the blame) on their God-appointed leaders.

Read Numbers 16:41–50.

Who did the people say had killed Korah and his followers? ______________

What did Moses tell Aaron to do in order to make atonement for the people's sinful rebellion?

____

In Week Six, Day Five, we learned that atonement carries the idea of covering over and brings back into harmony those who have been separated. We also found that incense symbolized prayer. As Aaron ran through the assembly carrying the censer, he was interceding for the people, and his prayers were like fragrant incense ascending to God. The Lord honored his chosen priest's prayers, and the deadly plague stopped. The day before, 250 censers arrogantly handled and invoked God's wrath. In contrast, one censer of incense honorably employed God's mercy.

Moses and Aaron consistently interceded on behalf of God's people. Read James 5:13–16 below and underline every situation in which these passages indicate we should pray:

> Is any one of you in trouble? He should pray. Is anyone happy? Let him sing songs of praise. Is any one of you sick? He should call the elders of the church to pray over him and anoint him with oil in the name of the Lord. And the prayer offered in faith will make the sick person well; the Lord will raise him up. If he has sinned, he will be forgiven. Therefore confess your sins to each other and pray for each other so that you may be healed. The prayer of a righteous man is powerful and effective.

How often do you intercede for others?

How often do you intercede for others? As a believer in Christ, you have been made right with God and are viewed as righteous in His sight. Your prayers are powerful and effective. You may not feel influential as you sit before the Lord and offer up what often seem like inadequate words, but God honors the prayers of His people. When your requests are in accordance with His will, your heavenly Father hears and responds (1 John 5:14).

You can make a difference in the lives of others through your faithful prayers on their behalf. On the lines below, list some people you know who are currently in need of prayer. Before you move forward with the rest of today's lesson, take a moment to intercede for those on your list. Their lives could be dramatically changed. The sick could very well be healed, and a rebellious soul just might turn back to the Lord.

Aaron passionately ran into the assembly with his censer, standing in prayer between the living and the dead. When the plague stopped, more than fourteen thousand bodies had to be buried in the desert. Moses and Aaron probably expected the Israelites to be grateful for the intervention and recognize Aaron as God's choice for His high priest. However, those Israelites appear to have been hardheaded as well as stiff-necked. Let's see how God settled the issue.

Read Numbers 17:1–13.

What happened to Aaron's staff as it was placed before the Lord in the Most Holy Place (v. 8)?

Scripture first mentioned Aaron's staff when he and Moses met with Pharaoh, back in Egypt. The wood of that staff had been dead for quite some time. Yet, when placed before the Lord, Aaron's staff didn't just sprout, it blossomed and produced almonds.

God's choice for high priest was once again made completely clear. Upon seeing Aaron's budding rod, the other tribal leaders silently took their staffs and walked away. The issue was settled. Aaron was the high priest.

God's choice for high priest was once again made completely clear.

What does Hebrews 5:1–4 tell you about the honor of serving God as a high priest?

God alone could appoint His high priest and Aaron was His choice. Serving as a priest was an honor, but the position also carried with it great responsibility. Read Numbers 18:1–7.

For what were Amram's family members responsible (including Moses) (v. 1)?

For what were Aaron and his sons responsible (v. 1)?

What gift did God give the priests to help them carry out their responsibilities (v. 6)?

Interestingly, God balanced the priests' responsibilities with another gift. Read Numbers 18:8, 20–24.

What "share and inheritance among the Israelites" did God give to the Levite's (v. 20)?

Israelites could enter the Tabernacle to worship and bring their offerings, but only the Levites would have the privilege of being near Him in the Tent of Meeting. The Lord was the Levites inheritance. God's gift to His servants was Himself.

What else did God give the Levites for the work they performed at the Tent of Meeting (v. 21)?

The priesthood itself was a gift to Aaron and his sons. The Levites were entrusted with the work of caring for the Tent of Meeting. It was a gift. The responsibilities were many, but God provided abundantly for the Levites and priests who served Him in the Tabernacle.

> The priesthood itself was a gift to Aaron and his sons.

God had an inheritance waiting for the other tribes as well. Read Numbers 26:52–56 and note the inheritance that awaited the other eleven tribes in their Promised Land:

The blossoms and almonds on Aaron's staff left no doubt as to God's choice for His high priest. As a gift to Aaron, the Levites were commissioned to assist him in caring for the Tent of Meeting. The Levites and priests had a special inheritance—God Himself. They also received the offerings and tithes from the Israelites. No other tribe had access to the Holy Place and the Most Holy Place in the Tent of Meeting. God also had good things in store for His nation. The other eleven tribes would each receive a share of the land of milk and honey when they eventually took possession of their Promised Land. Every tribe would receive good gifts from the loving hand of their merciful God.

> *Every good and perfect gift is from above, coming down from the Father of the heavenly lights, who does not change like shifting shadows. (James 1:17)*

WEEK NINE | **DAY THREE**

Death and Disappointment

But the Lord said to Moses and Aaron, "Because you did not trust in me enough to honor me as holy in the sight of the Israelites, you will not bring this community into the land I give them.

NUMBERS 20:12

Approximately forty years had passed since the Israelites were told to turn away from their Promised Land and head into the desert. God's people wandered from place to place as the fighting men who had been unwilling to battle for their Promised Land slowly died off. Moses endured whining and complaining and even a rebellious revolt led by his cousin, Korah. He witnessed conflict and resolved disputes. Moses shepherded God's people through the entire, long journey.

Approximately forty years had passed since the Israelites were told to turn away from their Promised Land and head into the desert.

As today's lesson begins, God's people have settled into a new camp at Kadesh in the Desert of Zin, which was located just south of the Promised Land.

Read Numbers 20:1–5.

Moses was now 120 years old. It must have been discouraging to listen to people whine and issue the same faithless complaints for forty years. I imagine their elderly leader's patience was wearing about as thin as the soles on his well-traveled sandals.

According to verse 1, what significant loss did Moses experience after the people got settled in Kadesh?

I imagine big-hearted Moses probably did a little reminiscing at Miriam's burial. She had been there at the bank of the Nile when little three-month old Moses was discovered by the Egyptian princess. It was Miriam who had suggested one of the Hebrew women nurse Moses. God used Miriam to orchestrate events so the young prince-to-be could spend several years with his Hebrew family. His sister Miriam had been a constant presence in his life. I can't help but wonder if Moses asked the women to close out his sister's burial service by dancing with tambourines in Miriam's honor (Exodus 15:20).

However it played out, Moses apparently didn't have much time to grieve or process his loss. The grumbling Israelites were once again in need of water and, thankfully, Moses knew where to go in order to meet that need.

Read Numbers 20:6–13.

According to verse 12, what did God say Moses failed to do and what was the consequence?

____

____

We once again are confronted with some tough passages to read and accept. Moses had endured years of complaining and grumbling. He had begged God to forgive these people over and over again. He had done his best to lead and complete the work God had called him to do. He made mistakes along the way, but this time, Moses' actions brought dire consequences. His dream of leading God's people into the Promised Land came crashing down on that water-gushing rock in Kadesh.

We once again are confronted with some tough passages to read and accept.

I wish I had a neat and tidy answer for why Moses was banished from the Promised Land. I do not. However, I do think there are some principles we can glean from this tragic event at Meribah that might help us avoid some divine discipline as **we** seek to follow God.

<u>1. Obeying God's commands is important.</u>

What did the Lord tell Moses to do to bring water out of the rock (v. 8)?

____

____

What did Moses do to the rock (v. 11)?

____

Moses angrily struck that rock and grumbled at the crowd rather than following God's instructions. The Lord still chose to provide water for the people, but Moses' disobedience was not overlooked.

Hold your place in Numbers, then read the following passages and note what you learn about the importance of obeying God's commands.

1 Samuel 15:22: _______________

2 John 1:5–6: _______________

According to Mark 12:28–31, what commands did Jesus say were the most important?

____

____

Your obedience to God's commands is an act of love that pleases God more than any sacrifice or offering you can place before Him. Loving your neighbor is one of God's greatest commands.

> Your obedience to God's commands is an act of love that pleases God more than any sacrifice or offering you can place before Him.

<u>2. Speaking Unrestrained by God's Spirit is foolish.</u>

According to Numbers 20:10, what did Moses say to the Israelites?

____

____

Moses' words were harsh and condemning. Read the passage below and underline the reason it indicates trouble came upon Moses.

By the waters of Meribah they angered the Lord, *and trouble came to Moses because of them; for they rebelled against the Spirit of God, and rash words came from Moses' lips. (Psalm 106:32-33)*

The Hebrew word translated, "rash" in verse 33 means "to babble; hence to vociferate angrily: pronounce; speak unadvisedly" (Strongs Concordance). In other words, in a fit of rage, Moses angrily screamed at the Israelites, allowing harsh words to flow from his lips unrestrained.

Have you ever gotten worked up and angrily spewed hurtful words at another person without restraint? I won't have you answer that question on the pages of our study, but I would guess most of us can recall a time when we've spoken rash, harsh words in anger that wounded people around us. What do the following passages say about the power of our words?

Proverbs 18:21: ______________________________

Proverbs 25:11: ______________________________

James 3:5–7: ______________________________

Take a moment to confess and seek forgiveness for those times when you have spoken unrestrained or harsh words and then ask God to help you, through the power of His Holy Spirit, to avoid speaking rashly or unadvisedly in the future. Write a brief prayer:

____

____

____

<u>3. Stealing God's glory is dangerous.</u>

Look again at Numbers 20:10. Who did Moses say was bringing the water from the rock?

____

Moses took credit for God's miraculous work as he screamed those harsh, unloving words to the people God had entrusted to his care.

Read Isaiah 42:8. What does God clearly state about His glory?

____

____

Moses blew it that day at Meribah. Apparently, Aaron jumped on Moses' glory-stealing bandwagon because the Lord said neither of them would enter the land of Canaan (Numbers 20:12).

Let's see what happened as the Israelites set out from Kadesh. Please read Numbers 20:22–29. What happened atop Mount Hor?

What an intimate moment for Aaron, Moses, and Eleazar. Without saying anything to the Israelite community about the purpose of their hike up Mount Hor, the three men did as the Lord commanded. I imagine Moses and Aaron said a prayer for Eleazar before placing the official garments of the high priest upon him. Moses and Aaron knew these were their last moments together. Eleazar was well aware his father was being "gathered to his people."

Have you ever spent time with someone who knew his or her time on earth was quickly coming to an end? I spent a lot of time with my Aunt Cheryl during her last few days on earth. Every conversation was steeped in meaning and purpose. Because of long-standing issues, our families hadn't been in touch in years. At the time, she was the only other committed Christian I knew of among my relatives. As the hours ticked by in her hospital room, we caught up on major events from years past. We laughed, cried, and talked about God's faithfulness in all our circumstances. Apologies were spoken. Forgiveness granted. Regrets dismissed. It was a deeply intimate time.

> Have you ever spent time with someone who knew his or her time on earth was quickly coming to an end?

The final moments of Aaron's life must have also been profoundly intimate. Apologies were probably spoken, forgiveness granted, and regrets dismissed. I imagine that goodbye conversation brought Aaron and Moses peace and Eleazar comfort. Moses and his nephew buried Aaron atop Mount Hor and then returned to the Israelite community for an official time of mourning.

Today's lesson was filled with death and disappointment. Please don't be discouraged. Press on and finish our last few lessons of this study of Moses. We still have a few more lessons to learn from this Old Testament legend.

WEEK NINE DAY FOUR

Plots and Provocations

They were the ones who followed Balaam's advice and were the means of turning the Israelites away from the Lord in what happened at Peor, so that a plague struck the Lord's people.

NUMBERS 31:16

After mourning Aaron's death, the people left Mount Hor and traveled from place to place until they eventually arrived at the border of Moab. There they were attacked by a group of people called the Amorites. The Lord empowered His people to kill the Amorite king, Sihon, and take over their land. The Israelites were then confronted by the people of Bashan, a nearby territory, but were also able to kill Bashan's king, Og, to secure that land as well.

Begin today by reading Deuteronomy 3:21–29.

What fervent plea did Moses make of God?

How did the Lord respond?

Moses' requests were met with a clear, "no." His time as Israel's leader was short and, sadly, he would only get the opportunity to see the Promised Land from a distance. I imagine Moses was downhearted as the Israelites settled in the valley of Beth Peor. However, he didn't have much time to feel sorry for himself. The Israelites continued north and camped at a town named Shittim, which was across the Jordan River from Jericho. The king of Moab took notice of the invasion upon his territory, but rather than confront the massive group as the other kings had done, Moab's king decided to take a less direct approach to eliminating this threat from his land.

Read Numbers 22:1–7.

What was Balak's strategy for defeating the Israelites (v. 6)?

What elders did the Moabites recruit to join them in their effort to defeat the Israelites (v.4)?

The people from Moses' former stomping grounds were now conspiring against him. Thankfully, the plot didn't work. God made sure Balaam pronounced a blessing over Israel rather than a curse. Unfortunately, a new plan was formulated that was far more successful.

Read Numbers 25:1–5.

Look closely at verse 2. What did the people do at the idol worshipping celebration that might have made the prospect of joining the Moabites quite enticing to our desert wandering, manna eating Israelites?

The Moabites had a feast, as they sacrificed to the idol known as Baal of Peor. Faced with the temptation of a celebratory spread of food and women seductively offering themselves as the main course, many of the men of Israel fell to the temptation and worshiped Baal on Mount Peor.

According to Numbers 31:15–16, who came up with the plan for the Moabite women to seduce the men of Israel, and what was the intended purpose?

The Israelites were set up, and they walked right into the trap. Evidently, Balaam told the Moabites to have their women lure the Israelites away from the Lord. Let's keep reading and see how this incident played out.

Read Numbers 25:6–18.

Moses stood before the assembly and announced that the judges would have to kill all of the men who had worshipped Baal of Peor. Evidently, a plague once again began to spread throughout the camp. The circumstances were so dire that the whole assembly was weeping in front of the Tent of Meeting. As the scene was unfolding, Zimri had the audacity to walk right past Moses, escorting a Midianite woman to his tent.

According to verse 18, who was Cozbi?

What did Eleazar's son, Phinehas, do that caused the deadly plague to cease (v. 8)?

What did the Lord tell Moses to do as a result of this "affair of Peor" (v. 17)?

Now that had to be a difficult command for our family-oriented leader to follow. He'd spent forty years caring for sheep in Midian. His wife Zipporah was a Midianite. His sons were half-Midianite. Moses must have been conflicted over the Lord's directive to kill the Midianites. However, although he certainly wasn't flawless, simple, plain Moses had become reverently responsive to what God said (Isaiah 66:2 MSG). He chose to obey his Lord.

> Moses must have been conflicted over the Lord's directive to kill the Midianites.

Read Numbers 31:1–12.

Who did the Israelites kill in addition to the Midianites (v. 8)?

Moses sent twelve thousand Israelites to take revenge on the Midianites. They killed every man in Midian, along with five kings. While they were at it, they took the opportunity to slay Balaam for coming up with the plot that led to the deaths of twenty four thousand Israelite men. It was the final battle before Moses went to be with Yahweh, the Lord he had faithfully followed and served all those years in the desert.

This Day Four discussion has involved quite a bit of reading, but let's read one final passage as a review of Moses' journey with the Israelites.

Read Psalm 106:7–33.

Summarize verse 13 in your own words:

____

____

As we close the pages of our study at the end of Lesson Ten, may we never forget all that God did for the Israelites along their journey. May we remember the Lord's faithfulness in the past so we can more fully trust Him for our future. Let's remain true to our God. Anything else that bids for His place in our hearts is simply a lifeless idol.

As we close the pages of our study at the end of Lesson Ten, may we never forget all that God did for the Israelites along their journey.

These things happened to them as examples and were written down as warnings for us, on whom the fulfillment of the ages has come. (1 Corinthians 10:11)

WEEK NINE | **DAY FIVE**

Personal Application

Application for Day One

In Day One of this lesson, Moses was once again confronted by envy-driven discord, which, by the way, has no place within a community of faith. As a Levite, Korah was part of the privileged tribe who cared for the Tabernacle and worked near Yahweh in the Tent of Meeting. Korah's clan was assigned the honor of carrying God's holy furnishings, as His people traveled from one location to another. I would guess Korah would have been satisfied—even honored—with the place of service God had assigned to him had he not looked around and compared his duties with those of Moses and the priests.

Look at Numbers 18:7 below. How is the service of the priesthood described?

But only you and your sons may serve as priests in connection with everything at the altar and inside the curtain. I am giving you the service of the priesthood as a gift. Anyone else who comes near the sanctuary must be put to death. (NIV)

Sadly, thousands of years later, God's people still envy the gifts God chooses to give to His people. Like Korah, members of the body of Christ look around at the spiritual gifts of their peers and begin to make comparisons. Sometimes discord develops as one member of a church covets the spiritual gifts of another brother or sister in Christ.

Sadly, thousands of years later, God's people still envy the gifts God chooses to give to His people.

Read 1 Corinthians 12:4–7. According to verse 7, what is the reason God gives spiritual gifts to His people?

Now read 1 Corinthians 12:8–12 and note what else you learn about the reason God gives varying gifts to His followers:

Application for Day Two

After Korah and his followers were consumed by fire from the Lord or swallowed up by the very ground upon which they stood, it appears that the dispute over which tribe should receive the gift of the priesthood continued.

God told Moses to gather a staff from the head of each of the twelve tribes of Israel and place them before the Lord in the Tent of Meeting. God told Moses the staff of the man He chose for the priesthood would sprout.

What happened to Aaron's staff? (See Numbers 17:8)

God had given the privilege of serving Him at the Tabernacle to the tribe of Levi, represented by Aaron. In addition, God gave the gift of the priesthood to Aaron and his sons. There was no place for envy or division among the tribes over God's gift then, and there isn't any place for gift-envy among the church today.

Read through the spiritual gifts listed in 1 Corinthians 12:8–12, 27–28. Of the spiritual gifts listed, which ones do you think God has given to you?

As a believer in Christ, you are entrusted with spiritual gifts, and just as Aaron and the Levites had responsibilities that went along with the gifts they had received, you also have the responsibility to faithfully use the gifts God has given you. If you are unsure about your spiritual gifts, ask some leaders you respect for assistance. There are numerous spiritual gift surveys online or your church leadership may have a recommended method for assessing your spiritual gifts. Sometimes, you have to plug in and try serving in different areas of your church to figure out your gifts. The main point for today is this: You have spiritual gifts that have been bestowed upon you for the common good of the body of Christ. You are responsible for using the gifts God has given you for God's glory. There is no place for gift-envy among believers.

If you are unsure about your spiritual gifts, ask some leaders you respect for assistance.

Application for Day Three

In Day Three, Moses experienced some devastating losses. The lesson began with the death of Miriam, followed by Moses' angry outburst at Meribah, and closed with the death of Aaron atop Mount Hor. Because Moses and Aaron failed to honor God "as holy" before the Israelites, both men were stripped of the privilege of entering the Promised Land.

I don't understand all of the reasons God punished Moses so severely for his actions at Meribah, but one point seems abundantly clear. Obedience to God's commands is vitally important.

Do you remember what two commands Jesus said were most important? (Look back at Mark 12:30–31 for help.)

To continue our theme of utilizing our spiritual gifts, read 1 Corinthians 12:31—13:3.

As we exercise our spiritual gifts, what should be our ultimate focus?

Read 1 Corinthians 13:4–7, which give us a picture of what love looks like in action. If you are using your spiritual gifts in the body of Christ, what are some practical ways you can apply this description of love to the specific work you are doing at this time?

If you aren't currently serving, use these lines to write a prayer, asking God to help you discover your spiritual gifts and utilize them in a way that displays His love for others in the body of Christ.

Application for Day Four

Israel fell to temptation, as the Moabites seduced some of the Israelite men, luring them away from their devotion to Yahweh. The events that happened during the Israelites' time in the wilderness are recorded to help us recognize God's expectations for His people and to prepare us for the kinds of temptations we might face as we aspire to follow God and serve Him, using our spiritual gifts.

Read 1 Corinthians 10:1–13.

Write verse 12 in your own words:

We will all face temptation, and there is no temptation that is so extraordinary or powerful that we are not able to stand up against it with God's help.

We will all face temptation, and there is no temptation that is so extraordinary or powerful that we are not able to stand up against it with God's help. Thankfully, He will never allow us to be tempted beyond what we can bear.

Step back for a moment and pretend someone else is utilizing the spiritual gifts you have been given. Look back over 1 Corinthians 10:6–10 and note the types of temptations that might lure someone in your position away from true devotion to Yahweh:

If you seek God whenever you feel tempted, what does verse 13 tell you He will faithfully provide?

Watch and pray so that you will not fall into temptation. The spirit is willing, but the body is weak. (Mark 14:38)

Week 10

Ending Well

WEEK TEN | DAY ONE

Preparing for an Inheritance

The Lord said to Moses, "The land is to be allotted to them as an inheritance based on the number of names."

Numbers 26:52-53

Last week we studied highlights from the Israelites' forty-years of wandering in the desert. We ended with the reminder that the material we have studied was written for our benefit—to serve as a warning to us about the dangers of becoming rebellious or falling to temptation. Life is full of temptations. Thankfully, our God will never allow us to be tempted beyond what we can bear. He will be faithful to provide a way out so we can remain standing (1 Corinthians 10:13).

After the deadly plague ended in Moab, the Lord had Moses and Eleazar take a new census of the Israelite men who were twenty years or older in each of the twelve tribes.

Begin today by reading Numbers 26:1–4.

We won't read through the data from the entire census, however, since Moses is believed to have authored the book of Numbers. Read Numbers 26:7–11 and note what information he chose to include along with the census data:

One of the benefits we gain by studying the Old Testament is a greater understanding of the events we read about throughout Scripture. This incident involving Korah, Dathan and Abiram is a great example. If we weren't familiar with the story, Moses' writings about Korah might seem like insignificant data listed within this census. Instead, we know what these men did, and the fact Korah's family didn't die along with him is interesting and meaningful. In fact, look at 1 Chronicles 6:31–33, 37. What important position did Korah's descendant, Herman, hold many years later at the Tabernacle?

One of the benefits we gain by studying the Old Testament is a greater understanding of the events we read about throughout Scripture.

Look at the titles for Psalms 45—49 in your Bible. To whom are those psalms credited?

By learning the Old Testament stories, passages like these come to life. We discover that Korah's family "did not die out" because they chose not to stand with him during his rebellion against Moses and Aaron. Korah's family went on to make important contributions to the work at God's sanctuary. I can't help but wonder what works were never accomplished because Dathan and Abiram involved their families in their sin. It is a question only God can answer.

Let's get back to the census. Look at Numbers 26:51. How many men over twenty years old were counted?

After Moses counted the fighting men from each tribe, God relayed further instructions for his people to follow after they took possession of their land.

Please read Numbers 26:52–65. Which male Levites were counted (v. 62)?

The Levites were not fighting men; they were worshiping men. Every male Levite was counted, even the children, and each clan had assigned duties at the Tabernacle. They would not receive their own land in the Promised Land. Instead, God Himself was their inheritance along with the tithes of Israel (Numbers 18:20–21).

Look back at Numbers 26:64–65. Of all the men twenty years old or more who were counted in the census forty-years earlier, which men were still living at the time of this new census?

God had kept His Word. Other than Caleb and Joshua, not one of those fighting men who refused to believe God were still living.

God had kept His Word. Other than Caleb and Joshua, not one of those fighting men who refused to believe God were still living.

Interestingly, the death of one man in particular might have led to the extinction of his family name if it weren't for his five resourceful daughters who brought their father's case to the attention of Moses and Eleazar.

Read Numbers 27:1–4 and note the solution these women proposed?

Let's see how Moses responded to their request. Please read Numbers 27:5–11.

Inheritance was usually passed from one generation to the next through male offspring, but Zelophehad left behind only daughters. What point did the women bring up to substantiate the legitimacy of their request to inherit their father's property (v. 3)?

In other words, Zelophehad hadn't committed any more extraordinary sin than the rest of his generation that was sentenced to die in the desert. His daughters wanted to honor their father's memory by maintaining land for his descendants. Confronted with this unprecedented request, Moses took the case before the Lord and waited for an answer. God affirmed these women by allowing them to inherit their father's share of the Promised Land. He even went so far as to make this a permanent, legal directive for Israel.

According to Exodus 20:12, what was God's fifth commandment, and what was the reward for adhering to it?

These women weren't interested in gaining land for themselves. In that society, women were provided for through their husbands' families. Zelophehad's daughters sought to honor their father's memory. It doesn't surprise me at all that God granted their request.

Like Zelophehad's daughters, we need to do our best to honor our parents. Circumstances vary, and God's grace enables us to apply this command differently, based upon our circumstances. However, even if we don't feel our parents have lived in an honorable manner, we are still commanded to honor them. One way we honor our parents is by providing opportunities for our children to spend time with their grandparents. The memories that are created will ensure our parents will be remembered by future generations.

What are some tangible ways you have chosen to honor your parents?

What are some tangible ways you have chosen to honor your parents? If you struggle with this command, I encourage you to spend some time in prayer and ask God to show you some tangible ways you can honor your parents. Write your thoughts below:

Not long after Zelophehad's daughters were told they could inherit their father's land, some of the other family heads got concerned that when these women eventually married, this ruling would cause land allocated to the tribe of Manasseh to become the property of another tribe. The men brought their concern to Moses and the community leaders. Please read Numbers 36:1–13.

What restriction was placed upon Zelophehad's daughters if they wanted to inherit land and preserve their father's memory and how did they respond to God's mandate?

I imagine the anticipation was building as the Israelites were preparing for their inheritance. The people of Israel knew their Promised Land was just across the Jordan River. I would say Zelophehad's memory was indeed honored by his daughters' resourcefulness and willingness to comply with the Lord's commands. The former generation might have forfeited the chance to personally set foot on that land, but their sons and daughters were preparing to take possession of the land of milk and honey. It was an honor their fathers dreamed about when they followed Moses out of Egypt.

WEEK TEN DAY TWO

Passing the Staff

Moses said to the Lord, "May the Lord, the God of the spirits of all mankind, appoint a man over this community to go out and come in before them . . ."

NUMBERS 27:15–17

The next step in Israel's preparation for entering their Promised Land was the ordination of their new leader. Moses knew his remaining days on earth were few and, once again, his shepherd's heart was focused on the wellbeing of his oft rebellious flock. Let's eavesdrop on one of Moses' final conversations with the Lord.

Please read Numbers 27:12–17.

Moses asked God to appoint a man over the community so they wouldn't be like sheep without a shepherd. What do the following verses indicate happens when sheep are left without the leadership of a shepherd?

1 Kings 22:17: ______________________________

Zechariah 10:2: ______________________________

Matthew 9:36: ______________________________

In Ezekiel 34, the Lord rebuked the shepherds of Israel (a metaphor for Israel's leaders) because of their selfish, uncaring style of leadership. Read Ezekiel 34:1–6 and then summarize what you learn about the responsibilities of a shepherd.

____

____

____

What examples can you think of from the Israelites' time in the desert that might substantiate Moses' assessment that the Israelites were in need of a shepherd to "lead them out and bring them in"?

____

____

____

____

Now read Numbers 27:18–23.

According to verse 18, whom did God choose to be that Shepherd for Israel, and how is he described?

____

God's anointing and empowerment were transferring to Joshua. Israel's new leader had led the Israelites in battle (Exodus 17:8); he'd been on Mount Sinai with Moses (Exodus 24:13);

he'd witnessed Moses' intimate relationship with God (Exodus 33:11), and he'd been one of only two spies who believed the Israelites could conquer the giants of Canaan forty years earlier.

God's anointing and empowerment were transferring to Joshua.

Read Numbers 11:28. What experience made Joshua a logical choice for Israel's next leader?

____

What shepherding skills do you think Joshua might have learned in his role as Moses' aide?

____

____

____

Let's see how Moses commissioned Joshua. Please read Deuteronomy 31:1–8.

Moses' commissioning of Joshua serves as a beautiful example of how to transfer leadership from one leader to another. Moses had Joshua stand before Eleazar, the priest, and the whole assembly. He then laid his hands on Joshua, as the Lord commanded (Numbers 27:22–23). Moses transferred some of his authority to Joshua by publicly expressing his belief that his long-time aide was the man God had chosen as his successor. In essence, the staff of God was formally passed on to this newly appointed man of God.

Let's see what Moses did after he commissioned Joshua. Please read Deuteronomy 31:9–13.

What did Moses say the people were to hear publicly proclaimed every seven years after they settled in the Promised Land (v. 11)?

____

When Moses said, "this law", he was probably referring to the entire book of Deuteronomy. The Hebrew title for this book is translated "these are the words," and it is a record of Moses' sermons on the Law.[46]

After Joshua's public ordination, the Lord summoned he and Moses to the Tent of Meeting for a more personal commissioning. Please read Deuteronomy 31:14–23.

What did the Lord indicate his people would do after they took possession of the Promised Land (vv. 16 and 20)?

What did God say he would do as a result of their actions (v. 17)?

After that speech, if I had just been commissioned as Israel's new leader, I imagine I would have been looking around the Tabernacle for a chair to sit in before I passed out. What a disconcerting call to duty. Actually, Joshua may have indeed been a little shaken. What did the Lord command Joshua in verse 23?

After the revealing meeting with the Lord, Moses finished writing down the law and then presented it to the Levites with some specific instructions.

Read Deuteronomy 31:24–29. What were those instructions (v. 26)?

Moses appears to have been a little grumpy as he presented the book of the law to the Levites. Sometimes, the strongest indicator that our time in a leadership position has come to an end is a lack of patience with people's flaws or a lack of compassion for their circumstances. Have you ever had a sense that it was time to move out of a leadership position of some kind? If so, did your attitude change as you began to recognize the need to move on? Explain:

Moses passed the staff to his companion and aide, Joshua. I imagine Joshua accepted that staff with trembling hands. He had big sandals to fill. Thankfully, he had an even bigger God to empower him.

The Lord gave this command to Joshua son of Nun: "Be strong and courageous, for you will bring the Israelites into the land I promised them on oath, and I myself will be with you. (Deuteronomy 31:23)

WEEK TEN **DAY THREE**

Final Petitions

They are not just idle words for you—they are your life. By them you will live long in the land you are crossing the Jordan to possess.

DEUTERONOMY 32:47

In yesterday's lesson, Moses asked God to appoint a shepherd to take his place as leader over the community of Israel; someone to lead them out and bring them in (Numbers 27:17). God chose Joshua. The elderly leader commissioned Joshua publicly, and then God commissioned the new leader privately at the Tent of Meeting. Moses then finished writing down the law, probably the entire book of Deuteronomy, and entrusted it to the Levites, who carried the Ark of the Covenant during Israel's travels.

To begin today's lesson, let's look again at Moses' last conversation with God at the Tent of Meeting. Re-read Deuteronomy 31:19–22.

In this last conversation with God at the Tent of Meeting, what did God tell Moses to write down and teach to the Israelites and what purpose did it serve?

____

____

When our children were young, car rides included fun, upbeat children's songs filled with truths from God's Word. Those catchy tunes were a great way for us to hide God's word in our hearts (Psalm 119:11). One particular song recited the books of the Bible in order. Brandon and Brianna are now adults, but to this day that song immediately begins to replay in mind whenever I thumb through my Bible looking for a particular book. For some reason, it is easier to remember words or concepts when we sing them—and it is a lot more fun too.

God gave Moses a song to teach the Israelites so generations later, when they turned away from Him, the words would convict their wayward hearts. We won't read the entire song, but let's look at some of the imagery God used in this song to help us understand the concepts He wanted His people to remember.

Begin by reading Deuteronomy 31:30—32:2. To what does God compare His words?

___

Based on this beautiful imagery, how does God want His Word to impact His people?

___

___

What metaphor is used to describe God in Deuteronomy 32:3–4, and what image do you think He is communicating with His choice of this word?

___

___

I think of a strong, stable, immovable object. God wanted His people to remember He is a solid and permanent part of their lives; His ways are always just, and they could count on Him to be faithful through the ages.

Read Deuteronomy 32:10–11 from The Message below:

He found him out in the wilderness, in an empty, windswept wasteland.
He threw his arms around him, lavished attention on him,
guarding him as the apple of his eye.
He was like an eagle hovering over its nest, overshadowing its young,
then spreading its wings, lifting them into the air, teaching them to fly.

To what does God compare His watchful care over His people?

An eagle, by stirring up the nest, thrusts eaglets out into the air to try their wings, but doesn't leave them altogether to their own resources. The parent eagle catches the fluttering little ones on its outspread wings and again deposits them in the nest.[47] The generation of former slaves used to depend on the Pharaoh of Egypt for their daily rations. They had fearfully obeyed his every command. God used their time in the desert to re-train them to depend on the Lord alone for their provision and to help them learn to fear Him over all other gods (Exodus 18:11).

(Hold your place in Deuteronomy) What does Isaiah 40:28–31 say to those who trust in God to care for them?

Moses' song spoke of the day when the Israelites would take God's blessings of abundance in Canaan for granted, rejecting Him and turning instead to lifeless idols. God warned that He would then withdraw His eagle-like protection from Israel and that they would endure calamities and famine and plagues.

Read Deuteronomy 32:15–20 and summarize the scenario God's song predicted:

What does Proverbs 3:11–12 tell you about the Lord's discipline?

The discipline God brought upon His people throughout their journey in the desert was ultimately for the nation's good. Like a mother eagle training her young to fly on their own, God was preparing His people for life in their Promised Land.

The discipline God brought upon His people throughout their journey in the desert was ultimately for the nation's good.

Once there, He knew they would eventually take His provision for granted and abandon their relationship with Him. He knew they would turn to lifeless, powerless idols. When that happened, He would once again discipline them by withdrawing His protection so they would once again recognize their need for the one and only true God.

Read Hebrews 12:5–13. What do you learn about one of the purposes for our hardships and trials?

____

____

According to verse 7, how we are to view hardship? ____________________

I've openly shared with you that my family has endured a good deal of hardship this year as I've been writing this study. These lessons are humbling. We aren't disciplined unless we need correcting, so please know, I teach as one being taught. Seasons of hardship are difficult, but God disciplines so we may share in His holiness. The tough times refine us. So let's strengthen our feeble arms and weak knees. Let's ask God to help us to make level paths for our feet so we will come through our trials stronger and healthier.

Please read Deuteronomy 32:44–47.

What Moses he say about God's law (v. 47)?

____

____

____

The words of God's law are not just meaningless words written down by a passionate old man who led Israel for over forty years; they are life-sustaining principles for God's people. If the Israelites chose to live according to God's laws, they would live long and full lives in their Promised Land. Moses pleaded with God's people to remember those words and to live by them. It was His final petition as he prepared to say goodbye to them.

The words of God's law are not just meaningless words written down by a passionate old man who led Israel for over forty years; they are life-sustaining principles for God's people.

As we close today's lesson, take Moses' words personally. God's Word is life to you. Let's do our best to live according to God's Word. Let's be grateful for every good thing God bestows on us and let's treat hardship as discipline, trusting God to bring forth a harvest of righteousness and peace as we are trained by it.

> *Therefore, strengthen your feeble arms and weak knees. Make level paths for your feet, so that the lame may not be disabled, but rather healed. (Hebrews 12:12–13)*

WEEK TEN | DAY FOUR

Ending Well

This is the blessing that Moses the man of God pronounced on the Israelites before his death.

Deuteronomy 33:1

Today, we will watch a legend die well. After Moses made his final petitions to the people he had led and served for more than forty years, Israel's passionate leader was told his time on earth had come to an end. Please read Deuteronomy 32:48–52.

What mountain did God tell Moses to climb in order to view Canaan?

Mount Nebo was one of the more prominent peaks in the Abarim Range in Moab.[48] God told Moses to climb that mountain and view the Promised Land before he died. Knowing this was his last day on earth, Moses lovingly recited a blessing over the tribes of Israel, by name. In the Hebrew culture, it was customary for a father to speak a blessing over his children before he died. In the Old Testament, a blessing was a wish or prayer for things that were to come in the future.[49] In many ways, Moses was like a father to the Israelites. I imagine each person at the assembly waited for their tribe's name to be called and then carefully listened to the blessing Moses chose to speak over them. I have no doubt his words had great significance and were a source of encouragement for God's people.

When our daughter was in her junior year of high school, the faculty organized a ring ceremony, and parents were strongly encouraged to attend and to present their student with his or her senior ring. As part of the ceremony, parents were asked to pronounce a public blessing over their child. Each family stood at the front of the assembly and parents spoke words of approval and acceptance, stating their child's strengths and communicating a sense of anticipation for what God would do in and through them after their time in school was complete. It was a moving experience to see each student's reaction to those words of affirmation and praise spoken over them by their parents at that gathering of their peers.

Have you ever spoken a formal blessing over your children? If so, use the lines provided below to describe that experience. If not, I want to encourage you as a fellow parent to do so. I recommend writing the blessing down and reading it, perhaps at some sort of ceremonial gathering with extended family or friends. You might choose to speak that blessing over them to mark a milestone, such as a high school or college graduation. Based on my own experience, I truly believe that public blessing, filled with words of acceptance and love, will be a source of strength for your child and bonding for your family. Use the lines below to jot down some ideas for bestowing a blessing upon your child(ren).

Have you ever spoken a formal blessing over your children?

After Moses spoke that blessing over the Israelites, it was time for Israel's legendary leader to climb Mount Nebo. I feel a twinge of sadness as we come to these passages, as though I am about to say goodbye to a man I highly respect and whose leadership I have come to appreciate.

Read Deuteronomy 34:1–4. If you have a map of the territory allocated to the twelve tribes of Israel, I recommend glancing at it as you read.

In the NIV, verse 1 reads, "There the Lord showed him the whole land." God knew what territory each tribe would receive. He laid it all out for Moses there on the top of Mount Nebo. I imagine Moses was filled with a mixture of pleasure with God's allotment of the territory and disappointment that he would never personally witness the fulfillment of God's promise.

Look back at Deuteronomy 3:25. What request had Moses made of God?

The Lord graciously allowed Moses to see the "good land beyond the Jordan." As much as God loved Moses, His decision not to allow him to cross over and lead the Israelites into the Promised Land was final. However, God was right there with Moses, explaining (I would guess with enthusiasm) all that His people would inherit in the land flowing with milk and honey. I imagine God probably showed Moses the valley where those fine, ripe grapes were taken in the Negev. It must have been a poignant moment for Israel's legendary leader.

Now read Deuteronomy 34:5–9. Look closely at verses 5–6. Who buried Moses?

The last moments of Moses' life were spent in intimate fellowship with His God. After Israel's leader took his last breath, the friend of God was buried by Yahweh Himself.

Interestingly, it appears there was some sort of dispute in the heavenly realms over what should be done with Moses' body. Read Jude 9 and note what celestial beings were involved in this dispute:

Can you think of a reason the devil would quarrel over what should be done with Moses' body?

I think we find a clue as to the evil one's agenda back in Deuteronomy 34:6. What does this passage say about Moses' grave?

> God's people were prone to worship idols. Had a man buried Moses, I suspect a shrine would have been erected in his honor.

God's people were prone to worship idols. Had a man buried Moses, I suspect a shrine would have been erected in his honor. Many Israelites probably would have worshipped their former leader, and people would still be visiting that gravesite today. I imagine Satan disputed with the Archangel Michael because he wanted that body to distract Israel from their devotion to God. Whatever was at the root of the argument, God took care of it by burying His servant Himself. There are many sites tourists visit over in that region every year, but we can rest assured Moses' grave won't be added to any tour.

What does verse 7 say about Moses' health at the ripe old age of 120?

I started wearing reading glasses in my early forties. Today, I can't stretch my arms out far enough to clearly read even my giant print Bible. Even driving has now become a challenge without glasses. Yet, at 120, Moses' eyes were not weak nor his strength gone. Now that is an amazing blessing.

This probably sounds quirky, but I enjoy reading tombstones. The words a family chooses to have written on their loved ones' graves speak volumes about a person's character and the type of life he or she lived during their brief time on this earth. Reading tombstones in a graveyard reminds me to make the most of my years here. Someday, someone will decide what to write on my tombstone. Now that is a humbling thought, isn't it?

For Moses there will never be a tombstone, but he will forever be remembered on the pages of our Bibles. Let's read what God chose to have written in honor of the man with whom He chose to speak as a man speaks with his friend.

Read Deuteronomy 34:10–12.

Now that passage speaks of a man who lived and died well!

Just in case you are concerned that this was the last of Moses, the Man of God made another appearance on a mountain in the pages of Scripture and I'd be remiss to exclude it. We'll visit those passages in Day Five and we'll venture into the Most Holy Place as we conclude our tour of the Tabernacle. I believe Moses would consider it a fitting end to our study as we once again enter the holy sanctuary and witness God's glory through the pages of His Word.

WEEK TEN | DAY FIVE

Glory Unveiled

This is love: not that we loved God, but that He loved us and sent His Son as an atoning sacrifice for our sins.

1 John 4:10

As Israel's legendary leader, Moses lived and died well. He served God for more than forty years, and "no prophet has risen in Israel like Moses, whom the Lord knew face to face" (Deuteronomy 34:10). As Israel's deliverer, Moses was a "type" (a foreshadowing of a future person or event) of Jesus. Moses delivered God's people from their physical slavery in Egypt; Jesus delivers all people (who choose to place their faith in Him) from slavery to their sinful natures. Moses led God's people to the promised land of their inheritance; Jesus leads God's people to their promised eternal inheritance.

As Israel's legendary leader, Moses lived and died well.

Scripture tells us Jesus made numerous appearances after His death and resurrection. Interestingly, Moses also made an appearance on earth after his death. Read Luke 9:28–32. At what significant event did Moses once again appear?

According to verse 31, what were Elijah, Moses, and Jesus discussing at this extraordinary meeting?

All the fullness of God was present in bodily form in the person of Jesus Christ. Moses had spent many a day talking with God at the top of mountains. He'd seen God's glorious splendor as bright and beautiful as Jesus appeared that day on the mount of transfiguration. Moses had been an eyewitness to God's glory throughout his life, however, the manifestation of God's active presence that people were about to witness in Jerusalem must have stirred up an array of emotions for Israel's big-hearted leader. Jesus was about to allow Himself to be nailed upon a cross for all sin. Moses knew Jesus would die so God's people could live. That knowledge must have brought back images from that amazing night in Egypt when God's people were covered and lives were spared by the blood of the Passover lamb. Jesus is our Passover Lamb (1 Corinthians 5:7). What other important roles does Jesus fulfill according to Hebrews 3:1?

As we learned in our study, Aaron and his sons were God's appointed priests. They served at the Tabernacle and then later at the temple. When one high priest died, a new one would be appointed from among Aaron's descendants. God appointed each high priest, and "Christ also did not take upon himself the glory of becoming a high priest" (Hebrews 5:5). God the Son was appointed by God the Father.

Read Hebrews 7:23–25 below. Underline the length of time Jesus' priesthood lasts and why.

There were many priests under the old system, for death prevented them from remaining in office. But because Jesus lives forever, his priesthood lasts forever. Therefore he is able, once and forever, to save those who come to God through him. He lives forever to intercede with God on their behalf (NLT).

According to Hebrews 7:26–27, what makes Jesus distinctive from the high priests who descended from Aaron?

Read Hebrews 8:1–2. Where does Jesus serve?

Now read Hebrews 9:11–12. By what means did Jesus enter the Most Holy Place in the "more perfect tabernacle"?

Read Hebrews 9:25–28

Our High Priest, Jesus Christ, entered the ultimate Tabernacle in heaven by His own blood shed on the cross, and by that sacrifice He made atonement (at-one-ment) for all sins and reconciled to God everyone who places their faith in Him.

In Week Six, we took a virtual tour (so to speak) of the earthly Tabernacle and found Jesus was depicted in each of the holy furnishings. We stopped our tour as we stood before the curtain that veiled the Most Holy Place where the Ark of the Covenant was housed. As we close our study, I'd like to complete that tour. Glance back at your diagram of the Tabernacle on page 115.

Let's begin with a reminder of how we gain access to the Most Holy Place. Read Mark 15:37–38 below and underline the description of what happened at the moment Jesus breathed His last breath:

With a loud cry, Jesus breathed his last. The curtain of the temple was torn in two from top to bottom.

If you recall from our study of the materials used to construct the Tabernacle, this curtain was not made of a thin piece of cloth. It was made of "yarn and finely twisted linen, with cherubim worked into it" (Exodus 26:31).

I don't want to contradict Scripture, but my mother was a professional decorator and designer for many years and she always corrected me whenever I called custom draperies, "curtains." She would abruptly say, "A curtain is a cheap piece of fabric, Mindy. These are draperies." This was indeed a drapery and, might I add, it would not be easily torn. Yet, when our eternal

High Priest and Passover Lamb breathed His last breath, that custom made elaborate drapery miraculously tore in two from the top to the bottom. The sin that had required that barrier to be established had been paid for with the blood of Jesus and everyone who believes in Him has full access to the Most Holy Place in the heavenly tabernacle where our Lord dwells. According to Psalm 99:1, where does God sit?

God sits enthroned between the two cherubim in His throne room—the Most Holy Place in His heavenly Tabernacle. Take a moment to bow before His throne and thank Him for the privilege of entering. Then step reverently between the two torn pieces of drapery, into the sacred inner sanctuary where you will find the Ark of the Covenant.

God sits enthroned between the two cherubim in His throne room—the Most Holy Place in His heavenly Tabernacle.

Read Exodus 25:21 below:

You shall put the mercy seat on the top of the ark, and in the ark you shall put the Testimony [the Ten Commandments] that I will give you. (Exodus 25:21 AMP)

How is the cover described in this verse? ____________________

Once again, Jesus Christ is depicted in this most holy furnishing in God's sanctuary. Turn to 1 John 4:10 and note how Jesus is described:

Whether your Bible refers to Him as the atoning sacrifice or the propitiation, the Greek word is ***hilasterion,*** and it means, "an expiatory (place or thing), an atoning victim, or specifically the lid of the Ark (in the Temple)—mercy seat, propitiation (***Strong's Concordance***).

Jesus ***is*** the mercy seat over the Ark of the Testimony in the Most Holy Place. He is the means by which we are reconciled with God and can have access to His active presence. Jesus is the source of mercy and grace and forgiveness for sin. You come before a holy God because of the atoning sacrifice of Jesus—the propitiation for our sins—the mercy seat of the Ark.

Jesus *is* the mercy seat over the Ark of the Testimony in the Most Holy Place.

For we do not have a high priest who is unable to sympathize with our weaknesses, but we have one who has been tempted in every way, just as we are—yet was without sin. Let us then approach the throne of grace with confidence, so that we may receive mercy and find grace to help us in our time of need. (Hebrews 4:15–16)

To conclude our tour, let's be so bold as to peek at the contents of the Ark.

To conclude our tour, let's be so bold as to peek at the contents of the Ark. Read Hebrews 9:3–4, and describe each item in the sacred Ark on the lines provided.

1). ______________________________

2). ______________________________

3). ______________________________

Could it be that these objects were kept below the mercy seat because each of these sacred items was a powerful reminder of God's abundant, underserved mercy? The Israelites whined and complained for forty years as they traveled with Moses through the desert. They refused to believe God would meet their needs and sometimes even questioned His presence with them. Yet, God mercifully provided manna every morning for more than forty years. Although the Israelite leaders rebelled against God's established authority and questioned His choice of Aaron for priest, God was merciful, confirming His choice with the budding rod of Aaron rather than bringing His wrath upon them as He had with Korah and his followers. God's people never were able to keep the law (represented by the Ten Commandments) and hold up their end of the covenant God established through Moses. Yet, God's mercy was evident as Jesus, our High Priest, became the atoning sacrifice and propitiation—the mercy seat—for all sin. In the course of our study, I pray you have gained a greater appreciation for God's mercy. For each time we enter His throne room by the blood of Christ, we are eyewitnesses to Glory!

Moses had asked God to forgive the "stiff-necked" Israelites over and over again during his forty-years in the desert. He passionately wanted all nations to know "The Lord is slow to anger, abounding in love and forgiving sin and rebellion" (Numbers 14:18). Moses had Aaron make atonement for Israel's rebellion (Numbers 16:46) and even asked God to "blot out" his name from His book in their place (Exodus 32:32). Our faithful protagonist often displayed a sacrificial love for God's people that resembled the sacrificial love of Jesus—our Passover Lamb, appointed High Priest, and glorious Mercy Seat in the throne room of our God.

As we end this study, write our definition of God's glory one more time (See p. 56 if you need help):

Reflect back over the past ten weeks of study. In what ways have you gained a great revelation of God's power and character?

Over the past ten weeks, we traveled with Moses through the various seasons of his life—his early years as the forbidden son of Hebrew slaves; his days as a somewhat prideful prince who murdered an Egyptian during his presumptuous attempt to rescue his people; his years as a lowly shepherd tending his father-in-law's flock. We watched Moses transform from an insecure, fearful shepherd, into the well-respected, legendary prophet and leader of Israel.

Over the past ten weeks, we traveled with Moses through the various seasons of his life. We watched Moses transform from an insecure, fearful shepherd, into the well-respected, legendary prophet and leader of Israel.

Moses' transformation was a manifestation of God's active presence. I trust that in the course of our study, you have discovered God's active presence as revealed in Scripture, but more importantly, I pray you have discovered His active presence in your life today. Each time you become aware of His activity in and around you, you, like Moses, are an eyewitness to glory.

END NOTES

1. William Whiston, ***Josephus, The Complete Works*** (Nashville, TN: Thomas Nelson Publishers, 1998), 77.

2. Michael Fishbane, ***The Jewish Study Bible*** (New York: Oxford University Press, Inc., 2004), 108.

3. H. L. Ellison, ***The Daily Bible Study Series: Exodus*** (Edinburgh, Scotland: The Saint Andrew Press & Louisville, KY and London, England: Westminster John Knox Press, 1982), 10.

4. William Whiston, A.M., ***Josephus: The Complete Works*** (Nashville: Thomas Nelson Publishers, 1998), 80.

5. Merrill C. Tenney, ***The New International Bible Dictionary*** (Grand Rapids, MI: Zondervan Publishing House, 1987), 525.

6. Ellison, 12.

7. John F. Walvoord and Roy B. Zuck, ***The Bible Knowledge Commentary: Old Testament*** (Colorado Springs, CO: Cook Communications Ministries, 2000), 111.

8. Ibid, 1178.

9. Ellison, 17.

10. Kenneth L. Barker and John R. Kohlenberger III, ***The Expositor's Bible Commentary, Abridged Edition Old Testament*** (Grand Rapids, MI: The Zondervan Corporation, 1994), 69.

11. Ibid, 72.

12. W. E. Vine, Merrill F. Unger and William White Jr., ***Vine's Complete Expository Dictionary of Old and New Testament Words*** (Nashville, TN: Thomas Nelson, Inc., 1996), 390.

13. Barker and Kohlenberger III, 71.

14. Religion in Ancient Egypt: The Gods and Goddesses <>http:ww/www.ancientegyptonline.co.uk/thegods.html

15. Walvoord and Zuck, 126.

16. Joseph Tabory, Bar-Ilan University, ***The Jewish Quarterly Review, LXXXVI, Nos.3–4 (January–April, 1996)*** (Center for Advanced Judaic Studies, University of Pennsylvania), 395–406

17. Walvoord and Zuck, 130.

18. Hebrew Lexicon http://www.biblestudytools.com/lexicons/hebrew/kjv/rapha.html

19. Barker and Kohlenberger III, 86.

20. Footnote a, ***NIV Thinline Reference Bible, Large Print*** (Grand Rapids, MI: Zondervan, 2005), 82.

21. Barker and Kohlenberger III, 96.

22. Herbert Lockyer, ***All the Men of the Bible*** (Grand Rapids, MI: Zondervan, Copyright by Herbert Lockyer, 1958), 151.

23. J. D. Douglas and Merrill C. Tenney, ***The New International Bible Dictionary*** (Grand Rapids, MI: Zondervan Publishing House, 1987), 113.

24. Douglas K. Stuart, ***The New American Commentary, Volume 2: Exodus*** (Nashville, TN: B&H Publishing Group, 2006), 414–415.

25. http://www.treasury.gov/about/education/Pages/in-god-we-trust.aspx

26. Walvoord and Zuck, 148.

27. Ibid, 150.

28. Douglas and Tenney, 231.

29. http://www.ancientegyptonline.co.uk/bullcult.html

30. Douglas and Tenney, 861.
31. Ibid, 108.
32. Ibid, 349.
33. Adele Berlin and Marc Zvi Brettler, ***The Jewish Study Bible, Jewish Publication Society*** (Oxford, New York: Oxford Press, 1999), 297.
34. Douglas and Tenney, 228.
35. Barker and Kohlenberger III, 195.
36. Ibid, 226.
37. Douglas and Tenney, 1061.
38. ***The Holy Bible, New International Version*** (International Bible Society, 1984, Grand Rapids, MI: The Zondervan Corporation, NIV Thinline Reference Bible, 2005), 164.
39. Whiston, 81–82.
40. Merrill F. Unger, ***Concise Bible Dictionary*** (Owings Mills, Maryland: Tyndale House Publishers, Inc., 1974), 54.
41. ***The New International Webster's Concise Dictionary of the English Language: International Encyclopedic Edition*** (Trident Press International, 1997), 237.
42. Douglas and Tenney, 273.
43. Walvoord and Zuck, 263.
44. Ibid, 229.
45. Lawrence O. Richards, ***New International Encyclopedia of Bible Words,*** (Grand Rapids, MI: Zondervan Publishing House, 1991), 512.
46. Walvoord and Zuck, 259.
47. Barker and Kohlenberger III, 279.
48. Walvoord and Zuck, 320.
49. Vine, Unger, and White Jr., 18.

Made in the USA
Middletown, DE
16 February 2024

49415455R00135